THE

SPIRITUAL GARDEN;

OR,

TRAITS OF CHRISTIAN CHARACTER DELINEATED

BY

HAMILTON, BURDER AND M'CHEYNE.

PHILADELPHIA:
PRESBYTERIAN BOARD OF PUBLICATION,

CONTENTS.

THE VINE

BY

THE REV. JAMES HAMILTON,

MINISTER OF THE FREE CHURCH, REGENT SQUARE,
LONDON.

"I am the True Vine."—JOHN XV. 1.

PHILADELPHIA:
PRESBYTERIAN BOARD OF PUBLICATION.

THE VINE.

Were you going early in the year to the banks of the Rhine, you would see the people on every slope, busied about some important plant. To your nearer view it looks little better than a wooden peg, a dead and sapless pin. But return in September, and you will find that the wintry peg has shot into a pillar of verdure, and from purple bunches is pouring fatness and fragrance on the soil. The shout of the vintage and the brimming vat explain the labours of the spring.

On the hills of Palestine the Heavenly Husbandman planted a goodly vine. But at first it had no form nor comeliness, and promised little. It was a root out of a dry ground, and few expected that it would come to any thing. And when its heavenly origin was hinted, in a rage the men of Nazareth cast it over their vineyard wall, and soon afterwards the men of Jerusalem took the tender Plant, and having bruised and trampled it under their indignant feet, they hoped that they had destroyed it for ever. But the Heavenly Husbandman did not lose sight of it. He planted it again. This time, however, he concealed it from view. He so contrived that though the branches were seen, the vine-stock should no longer be visible. Grafts might be joined to it and fruit might be gathered, but the stem itself was hidden.

A few weeks passed on, and a warm rain fell. A sweet and springy odour filled the air. It was the budding of the invisible Vine. It was the tender grape appearing. There were thousands of blossoms; and from year to year thereafter there was many a glorious vintage. And though rude days have followed; though the passengers have plucked it, and the persecutor has often scorched and torn the boughs, the Lord of Hosts will ere long return and visit this his Vine. He will cast out the heathen and plant it. He will prepare room before it, and cause it to take deep root and fill the earth. The hills of the Millennium will be covered with its shade, and the boughs thereof will be like the goodly cedars.

This earth was the land of the curse—it was the world of sin, death, and sorrow—when God sent his Son. He freighted the Mediator's person with life, righteousness, peace of conscience, and every mercy that a sinner needs. "As the Father hath life in himself, so did he give to the Son to have life in himself," (John v. 26;) and thus furnished with an abundance of life, he sent the Only-Begotten into the world. But the world hated him. It saw nothing attractive in him. It rejected the Saviour. It slew him. But God raised him again, and withdrew him out of mortal sight. Though now hidden from our view, he remains what he was during the days of his visible Incarnation. He is still the Saviour. He is still the sole Repository of heavenly blessings for our guilty and necessitous race. Though invisible, he is the great Vine-stock in which all merit and spiritual vitality reside. It is from his fulness that salvation is derived, and only from the grace that is in him that we can get any thing gracious. Though himself unseen, his members are visible. Believers are the branches of this wondrous Vine. At Pentecost they were freshest and fairest. They are, perhaps, equally numerous, but more sparse and straggling now. But to see the goodly Vine in its glory, we must wait till the present winter is past, and the summer of the earth is come; till for pardon and peace willing millions resort to Immanuel, and the rejected Root has become the Plant of Renown.

Those whom Christ originally addressed were fond of parables, and best understood such truths as were embodied in emblems and figures. But perhaps your mind has no turn for metaphor. You are rather confused than assisted by it. You have difficulty in following an allegory where people are com pared to the branches of a Vine; and when Christ speaks of a believer being a branch "in him," and of "abiding in him,"* you do not clearly apprehend it. But if you consider a little, you will easily make out the main idea. Christ compares himself to a Vine, and when you remember what a glad and lifesome tree it is, the tree through which vegetative life pours the fastest and most freely, and the tree with which the most refreshful and exulting associations were connected; and when you farther recollect that it was to bring abundance of life and felicity that Jesus came into the world, you can see how naturally in this tree of life Jesus found the emblem of himself. But this vine sapling which I hold in my hand—how is it to be made partaker of the life and fatness of the living vine? By creating the closest connexion possible. You engraft it. You take this leafless rod—perhaps severed from a wild vine—and you insert it in the quick vine-stock, and speedily the graft has taken. Fibre by fibre, and vein by vein the sapling clings and coheres, till the life of the tree is the life of this adopted branch, and the graft buds and blossoms and matures its clusters from the flowing juices of the vine. And Jesus has life in himself; he is now a man of joys; he knows that the Father loves

* See John xv. 1—10, a passage which it would be well to read over twice, so as fully to understand this tract.

him, and having completed the work given him to do, he rests again in the Father's bosom, secure in the Father's complacency, and most blessed for evermore. But here is a dead and sapless soul, here is a spirit to which holy joy is a stranger, and to which God is still unknown as a reconciled God and a loving Father. How is this dead and dreary soul to be made partaker of Christ's life and joy? By creating the closest possible connexion. That sapless twig lives when united to the Vine. That sinner lives when united to the Saviour. But what is the closest possible connexion between the sinner and the Saviour? It is such a connexion as joins soul to soul. It is such a connexion as joins the feeble and finite soul of the sinner, to the holy and Divine soul of the Saviour. It is such a union as confidence, and love, congeniality, and dependence, create. It is confidence—for Jesus died that he might bring us unto God, and when a soul is persuaded that Jesus is able to save to the uttermost, and resigns itself entirely to him as a sufficient Saviour—the soul which thus clings to Christ for salvation is by God regarded as one with Christ. A soul which trusts in the Surety will never come into condemnation, for the Surety would thereby be condemned; and a soul which cleaves to the Lord Jesus for pardon is justified already, for it is now part of that Substitute who was justified long ago. And it is love. You speak of souls that are knit together when they are affectionately attached to one another; and Christ and the Christian are joined by an intense, mutually-pervading, and death-surviving love. Accordingly, he himself calls this union a "continuance in his love." And it is congeniality. When tastes are identical, when persons love the same things and hate the same things, when desires move in concert, when the one treasures up the other's words and tries to anticipate the other's wishes, you say that hearts in such harmony are one spirit. And it is one spirit which fills Christ and the Christian—Christ's "words abide in him" (ver. 7.) There is many an endeared saying of his Lord hidden in his fondest memory And these sayings of Christ do not merely alight on him like rain on the vineyard, but live and abide in him like vital sap in the Vine. And these loved sayings and abiding words come out in new obedience, (ver. 10,) "If ye keep my commandments, ye shall abide in my love." And it is dependence. Where parties are united in any way to one another, one of whom is greatly superior in strength, or wisdom, or skill, it becomes natural and inevitable for the inferior to depend on the strength, or wisdom or skill of that other. Now the believer finds himself so weak, and ignorant, and sinful, that he is compelled to look to his Lord, in whom all these resources abound. Without Christ he can do nothing. But he has learned to lean on him, who of God is made to him wisdom, righteousness, and sanctification. Without Christ he cannot pacify an offended God; without Christ he cannot escape the curse of a broken law; without Christ he can do nothing to deliver himself from hell, nor secure his persevering progress to heaven; without Christ he cannot subdue a single sin nor overcome a single temptation. He discovers that it needs an Almighty power to sanctify. "It needs the same power to enlighten his understanding as gave sight to blind Bartimeus; it needs the same power to quiet his conscience, as said to the tempest, Peace, be still; it needs the same power to soften his hard and stony heart, as melted rivers from the rock; the same power to convert his carnal affections into spiritual, as changed the water into wine; the same to subdue his rebellious passions, as expelled the devils from the man possessed; and the same power to make him pure of heart and fit for glory, as made the leper clean." * And for all holy obedience, he verifies the saying of Jesus, "As the branch cannot bear fruit of itself, except it abide in the vine, no more can ye, except ye abide in me."

Wherever a soul believes in Jesus, loves him, is made one spirit with him, and depends on him for wisdom, strength, and righteousness, that soul is united to Jesus. That soul is *in* the Saviour, even as the branch is in the Vine; that soul is dear to God. It is ac-

* Clarkson's Sermons.

cepted in the Beloved, and becomes an ob ject of the Father's solicitude and care. And it will experience the benefits of this union. It will be fruitful; it will be purified; it will be powerful in prayer; for if union to Jesus be salvation, productiveness, sanctification, and prevalency in prayer are effects of this union which he himself has specified.*

1. The living branch is fruitful. The chemist who can analyze the fruit of the vine, finds many ingredients there. Of these, no single one, nor any two together, would form the juice of the grape; but the combination of all yields the polished and delicious berry, which every one knows so well. In different climates, and even in different seasons, the proportion and blending of these constituents may vary; but that is not a good cluster where any is wanting. The fruit of the true Vine has also been analyzed, and in the best specimens the nine following ingredients are found. (Gal. v. 22.)

LOVE, GENTLENESS,
JOY, GOODNESS,
PEACE, FAITH,
LONG-SUFFERING, MEEKNESS,
TEMPERANCE.

In poor samples there is a deficiency of one or other of these elements. A dry and diminutive sort is lacking in peace and joy. A tart kind, which sets the teeth on edge, owes

* John xv. 5, 2, 7.

its austerity to its scanty infusion of gentleness, goodness, and meekness. There is a watery deliquescent sort, which for the want of long-suffering is not easily preserved; and there is a flat variety, which having no body of faith or temperance, answers few useful purposes. Love is the essential principle which is in no case entirely absent; and by the glistening fulness and glad aroma which its plentiful presence creates, you can recognize the freshest and most generous clusters; whilst the predominance of some other element gives to each its distinguishing flavour, and marks the growth of Eshcol, Sibmah, or Lebanon.

(1.) Wherever there is union to Christ, there is love. This, as we have said, is the essential principle. Whatever else there be, if there be not love, it profits nothing, it proves nothing. Love to God and our neighbour is the essence of piety. It is the body, the basis, the staple element; and if the great commandment, and the next greatest be absent, whatever else there be, there is not Christianity. Brethren, have you got it? To Christ's question, "Lovest thou me?" is it your answer, "Lord, thou knowest all things, thou knowest that I love thee?" Then, if you love Jesus, you will love him whose express image Jesus is. To God in Christ, your soul will be attached in gratitude, submission, and complacency. You will not wish him less holy, less righteous, less true. Awed by his glorious majesty, and melted by his ineffable mercy, all that is dust and ashes in you will be humbled, and all that is filial will be inflamed. If nothingness and sin bid you be silent, the sight of your Saviour gone back to the bosom of his God and your God, awakens a cry of relenting tenderness, and adoring astonishment. Boldest where you are most abased, from the foot of the cross, the view of a reconciled God elicits the cry, Abba, Father. You love Him, who first loved you, and "feeling it sweet to be accepted of God on any grounds, to be accepted in his own beloved Son, you feel is sweeter far." *

(2.) And joy. The essence of love is attachment. Joy is the happiness of love. It is love exulting. It is love aware of its own felicity, and rioting in riches which it has no fear of exhausting. It is love taking a look of its treasure and surrendering itself to bliss without foreboding. "God's promises appear so strong, so solid, so substantial, more so than the rocks and everlasting hills; and his perfections, what shall I say of them? When I think of one, I wish to dwell upon it forever; but another, and another equally glorious, claims a share of admiration; and when I begin to praise, I wish never to cease, but to find it the commencement of that song which will never end. Very often have I felt as if I could that moment throw off the body, without first going to bid them fare-

* Nevins' Remains, p. 27.

well *that* are *at home* in my house. Let who will be rich, or admired, or prosperous, it is enough for me that there is such a God as Jehovah, such a Saviour as Jesus, and that they are infinitely and unchangeably glorious and happy!"* And in a similar frame another felt, "Were the universe destroyed, and I the only being in it besides God, He is fully adequate to my complete happiness; and had I been in an African wood, surrounded by venomous serpents, and devouring beasts, and savage men, in such a frame I should be the subject of perfect peace and exalted joy.†"

(3.) Peace. If joy be love exulting, peace is love reposing. It is love on the green pastures, it is love beside the still waters. It is that great calm which comes over the conscience, when it sees the atonement sufficient, and the Saviour willing. It is unclouded azure in a lake of glass. It is the soul, which Christ has pacified, spread out in serenity and simple faith, and the Lord God, merciful and gracious, smiling over it.

(4.) Long-suffering. This is love enduring. If the trial come direct from God, it is enough. It is correction. It is his heavenly Father's hand, and with Luther, the disciple cries, "Strike, Lord, strike. But, oh! do not forsake me." If the trial come from Christian brethren, till it be seven-fold seventy times

* Payson's Life, chap. 19.
† Memoirs of Rev. S. Pearce.

repeated, love to Jesus demands forgiveness. If it come from worldly men, it is the occasion for that magnanimity which recompenses evil with good. And in every case, it is an opportunity for following a Saviour, whom sufferings made perfect. That Saviour never loved the Father more intensely, than when his Father's face was hid, and when the bitter cup proclaimed his justice terrible, and his truth severe. One apostle denied him, and all the disciples forsook him; but Jesus prayed for Peter, whilst Peter was cursing, and his love followed the rest, even when they were running away. Jerusalem killed him; but in foresight of the guilty deed, it was over Jerusalem that Jesus wept, and when the deed was done, in publishing pardon and the peace of God, it was at Jerusalem that evangelists were directed to begin.

(5.) Gentleness, or affectionateness (χρηστοτης). This is love in society. It is love holding intercourse with those around it. It is that cordiality of aspect, and that soul of speech, which assure us that kind and earnest hearts may still be met with here below. It is that quiet influence which, like the scented flame of an alabaster lamp, fills many a home with light, and warmth, and fragrance all together. It is the carpet, soft and deep, which, whilst it diffuses a look of ample comfort, deadens many a creaking sound. It is the curtain which from many a beloved form, wards off at once the summer's glow, and the winter's wind. It is the pillow on which sickness lays its head and forgets half its misery, and to which death comes in a balmier dream. It is considerateness. It is tenderness of feeling. It is warmth of affection. It is promptitude of sympathy. It is love in all its depth, and all its delicacy. It is every melting thing included in that matchless grace, "the GENTLENESS of Christ." (2 Cor. x. 1.)

(6.) Goodness or beneficence. Love in action, love with its hand at the plough, love with the burden on its back. It is love carrying medicine to the sick, and food to the famished. It is love reading the Bible to the blind, and explaining the Gospel to the felon in his cell. It is love at the Sunday class, or in the Ragged school. It is love at the hovel door, or sailing far away in the missionary ship. But whatever task it undertakes, it is still the same,—Love following his footsteps, "who went about continually doing good."

(7.) Faith. Whether it means trust in God, or fidelity to principle and duty, Faith is love in the battle field. It is constancy following hard after God, when the world drags downward, and the flesh cries, "Halt." It is zeal holding fast sound words when fervour is costly and sound words are obnoxious. It is firmness marching through fire and through water to the post where duty calls and the captain waits. It is Elijah before Ahab. It is Stephen before the Sanhedrim. It is Luther at Worms. It is the martyr in the flames. Oh, no! It is Jesus in the desert. (Matt. iv. 1—11.) It is Jesus in Gethsemane. It is Jesus on the cross. And it is whosoever pursuing the path, or finishing the work which God has given him, like the great forerunner, does not fear to die.

(8.) Meekness is love at school—love at the Saviour's school. It is Christian lowlihood. It is the disciple learning to know himself; learning to fear, and distrust, and abhor himself. It is the disciple practising the sweet but self-emptying lesson of putting on the Lord Jesus, and finding all his righteousness in that righteous other. It is the disciple learning the defects of his own character, and taking hints from hostile as well as friendly monitors. It is the disciple praying and watching for the improvement of his talents, the mellowing of his temper, and the amelioration of his character. It is the loving Christian at the Saviour's feet, learning of him who is meek and lowly, and finding rest for his own soul.

(9.) Temperance — love taking exercise, love enduring hardness, love seeking to become healthful and athletic, love striving for the mastery in all things, and bringing the body under. It is superiority to sensual delights, and it is the power of applying resolutely to irksome duties for the Master's sake. It is self-denial and self-control. Fearful lest it should subside to gross carnality, or waste away into shadowy and hectic sentiment, temperance is love alert and timeously astir; sometimes rising before day for prayer, sometimes spending that day on tasks which laziness or daintiness declines. It is love with girt loins, and dusty feet, and blistered hands. It is love with the empty scrip but the glowing cheek—love subsisting on pulse and water, but grown so healthful and so hardy, that it "beareth all things, believeth all things, hopeth all things, endureth all things."

Reader, if you abide in Jesus—if His words abide in you, you will be neither barren nor unfruitful. Graces such as these will be in you, and abound. Is it so? The great vine-principle, the main element of the Christian character, holy love, does it abound in you? And blending with it, colouring it and sweetened by it, can you detect from time to time, joy in God, peace of conscience, patience in suffering, and forgiveness of injury, affectionateness, beneficence, trust in God, and trustworthiness in your place and calling, a lowly willingness to learn and readiness to take up the cross and deny yourself? When Christians live close to Christ his mind is transfused into theirs. "Purity and love shine forth in their character; meekness and truth guide their footsteps. Nay, in the experience of some, so great has been the change, that the very expression of their countenance has altered. Thus was it with Moses and Stephen. These blessed saints were full of God; Christ was in them of a truth; and his likeness was thus by them peculiarly reflected. Nor is it wonderful that such should sometimes be the case with believers; for, when he thus fills their hearts with his presence, when his peace dwells there; when the calm joy which he felt when rejoicing in spirit, reigns there; there must needs be gentleness in their manners, and heavenliness in their talk, and meekness in their eye, and angelic serenity and conscious elevation in their whole countenance." *

2. Every fruitful branch is purged. "The husbandman purgeth it that it may bring forth more fruit." It is the propensity of even fruitful branches to wanton into excessive foliage. But besides spoiling the appearance of the vine, the sap spent on the leaves is stolen from the grapes, and the excessive shade keeps out the sun. The husbandman prunes these shoots and suckers away, and while he makes the branch more sightly, he lets the noon-beams freely in, and makes the clusters richer. So is it with the sincerest Christians. In prosperous weather, when all goes well with them, they are apt to flaunt out in worldliness, and luxury, and pride. They grow selfish. They study their own ease. They seek great things for themselves. And the Husbandman, watchful and considerate, consulting his own glory and the fruitfulness of the vine, the Husbandman comes, and with the pruning shears of some afflictive providence, lops the deforming shoots away.

* "Thoughts on Union to Christ," by Sosthenes.

"Man's chief end is to glorify God, and enjoy him for ever." This was the thought which conveyed reproof and new quickening to a most amiable Christian,* after her greatest bereavement. "I felt that for the last twelve years I had misunderstood the great object for which I was made; that, if not my chief, a very high end with me had been to be happy in my husband, and make him happy in me. But now I felt that the highest happiness of a rational mind ought to arise, from answering the purpose for which God made it; and therefore that I ought to be happy in glorifying God, and not in enjoying myself." And it is to this result that every trial with which God visits his people is tending. It is to shut them up to His service as their chief end, and to Himself as their chiefest joy. It is not to hurt but to heal the tree that the Husbandman handles the pruning-hook. In deep dejection of spirit, Mr. Cecil was pacing to and fro in the Botanic Garden at Oxford, when he observed a fine specimen of the pomegranate almost cut through the stem. On asking the gardener the reason, he got an answer which explained the wounds of his own bleeding spirit. "Sir, this tree used to shoot so strong, that it bore nothing but leaves. I was, therefore, obliged to cut it in this manner, and when it was almost cut through, then it began to bear plenty of fruit." Ye suffering

* Mrs. Susan Huntington.

members of Christ, be thankful for every sorrow which weakens a lust or strengthens a grace. Though it should be a cut to the heart, be thankful for every sin and idol shorn away. Be thankful for whatever makes your conscience more tender, your thought more spiritual, and your character more consistent. Be thankful that it was the pruning knife and not the weeding hook which you felt: for if you suffer in Christ, you suffer with him; and if with him you suffer, with him you shall also reign. (2 Tim. ii. 12.)

3. A third consequence of abiding in Jesus is prevalency in prayer. "If ye abide in me, and my words abide in you, ye shall ask what ye will, and it shall be done unto you." One reason is that Christ's mind and the Father's agree, and Christ's mind is in the constant Christian. His will is merged in Christ's will; and instead of the petulant and unreasonable requests which worldly or divided hearts are apt to urge, a holy solicitude for God's glory predominates in his prayers. The first petition which his Master taught him, covers and qualifies all the rest; and whatsoever he may ask, he will not revoke the primary behest, "Our Father which art in heaven, hallowed be thy name." The believer who abides in Jesus, obtains answers to his prayers, because his sanctified will is apt to desire things according to the will of God. But more than this, abiding in Jesus is nearness to God. The man who

knows not how to use the Mediator's name, may pray from a sense of duty, or under the urgency of present distress. But if mere duty compel him, there is no comfort nor enlargement in the formal exercise; or if distress constrain him, coming as a stranger, there is no confidence in his approach, and he has no security that God has heard him. He stands in the empty vestibule, and without obtaining a glance of the Sovereign, at last leaves his petition, uncertain whether it shall ever reach its destination. The sinner who comes in the name of Jesus, is ushered at once to the Throne of Grace, and obtains the propitious ear of an all-sufficient God. And the sinner who abides in Jesus, who habitually comes in the Intercessor's name, finds in prayer, not only entrance to the palace of the King, but access to that Father whom Christ has taught him to regard with the affectionate security and tender reverence of a child. Prayer is his daily visit to his heavenly Father's dwelling—the hallowed chamber whose door the name of Jesus opens—the sweet and endeared closet where day by day he has told his griefs and fears, and wants and sins, and from which he has oft departed, rich in daily grace, and radiant in his heavenly Father's smiles.

Reader, beloved and longed for, have you understood these things? Do you not allow that your own soul is naturally fruitless and lifeless? Do you not confess that you have no more right to immortality, and no more power for holiness, than the severed sapling has power to blossom and bear fruit, so long as it abides alone? But do you equally perceive that Jesus is the true vine? Are you persuaded that there is so much life in Him that if you could only share his life, you would live also? so much merit in Him, that if it could only be made your own, you would be righteous also? so much holy energy in Him, that could it only be imparted to you, you too would have a spiritual mind, and delight in doing the will of God? Do you perceive that Christ Jesus is the great repository of justifying righteousness and sanctifying grace? Do you distinctly realize these two things—that you yourself are empty, and that in the Lord Jesus all fulness dwells?

But how is the empty scion to profit by the teeming Vine? How is a connexion to be created between the Mediator's fulness and your own vacuity? How is it that Christ and you shall become so truly one, that His beauty shall be on you and His spirit within you? We have already said that it is by believing him, loving him, copying from him, and depending on him. A shorter answer is his own. It is by letting Christ's word enter and abide. The disciples were made genuine, "clean," they got the real Vine-nature from the moment when they admitted Christ's words into willing hearts. And you too will be clean, the graft will strike, from the moment when you credit the word of Jesus. Should you credit that saying of Jesus, "God so loved the world that he gave his only begotten Son, that whosoever believeth in Him should not perish, but have everlasting life;" or should you comply with that other saying of Jesus, 'Come unto me, all ye that labour and are heavy laden, and I will give you rest;" should you abandon yourself to all the blessedness of believing what the True Witness says; should you suffer your weary soul this day to sink into the arms of that Saviour who rejoices to pardon and is mighty to save—the first entrance of such a word, and the first response of such a faith, would be the date of your better life, and the commencement of your union to Christ.

—The graft has taken. At first the juncture may be very slight, a single thread or fibre; and it is not till you try to part them that you find that they are knit together—that their life is one—and that the force which plucks away the graft must also wound the vine. And your faith may yet be no more than a single filament. It may be only one point of attachment by which you have got joined to the Lord Jesus. It may be only one solitary sentence — one isolated invitation or promise, of which you have got undoubting hold. But hold it fast. If it be the word of Jesus, cling to it. There is life in it, and, held fast, it will be life to you. One promise of Jesus credited, one invitation of Jesus accepted, is enough to make such union between Him and you, that the violence which sunders, if death to you, would be a bleeding heart to Him. Hold fast the faithful saying then, and as you cling to it, you will draw closer and closer to the living Vine. The surface of quick contact will enlarge, and as thread by thread, and vein by vein it widens, as word by word, and line by line the sayings of Jesus get hidden in your heart, the tokens of vitality will become to yourself and others, joyfully distinct. And though you may fear to-day that you have no interest in Christ—think no more of that; think of what He says. Believe him boldly; and as sure as He came into the world to save sinners, He will save you. Cleave to His assurances in all their breadth, and though you may feel yourself little better than a reprobate to day, you will be a saint in glory yet. And though you see no fruits of the Spirit yet, let Christ's word abide in you, and you will see them anon. And though you dread lest the faint hold you have got may end in a falling away, hold on till the feeble contact of this moment grow into a complete coalescence, and in joyful assurance of oneness with a sin-pardoning and sanctifying Saviour, you be able to exclaim, Who shall separate us from the love of Christ?

THE CEDAR

BY

THE REV. JAMES HAMILTON,

MINISTER OF THE FREE CHURCH, REGENT SQUARE, LONDON.

"The Righteous shall grow like a Cedar in Lebanon."—PSALM xcii. 12.

PHILADELPHIA:
PRESBYTERIAN BOARD OF PUBLICATION.

THE CEDAR.

Lebanon has sometimes been regarded as a type of Jesus Christ. Among surrounding mountains the loftiest and fairest, it may suggest to a devout and willing mind that Mighty One, who is fairer than all his fellows.* Its roots of everlasting rock, on the one side struck deep in Palestine, and on the other side reaching far into the Pagan lands, are like that righteousness, "great as the mountains," which the Son of God wrought out for the Jews and Gentiles,† and like the Rock of Ages himself, amidst his supremacy of power and wisdom, still partaker with his brethren. The streams of water trickling down its slopes, and gushing through its fragrant glens, may be a hint of heavenly influences, and of the Holy Spirit, through the Saviour's wounded side, flowing down to redeemed souls and onward to a widening Church. Its coronet of snow, glancing in

* Psa. xlv. 2. † Psa. xxxvi. 6.; Rom. i. 17.

G2

the sunny sky, is like that snowy hair *—the halo of enshrined Divinity, which marks the Son of Man in heaven—whilst its verdant ladder, linking heaven to earth, brings to remembrance the incarnation and Immanuel, "God with us." The corn which gilds its ample skirts, the vines which empurple its royal robe, and the starry blossoms which spangle it all over, may shadow the various joys which have sprung up the memorial of Messiah's advent. But it is not the corn nor the vine, nor the lily which is the glory of Lebanon. It is Lebanon growing and waving and scattering fragrance in the cedar—it is the vegetating rock—the arborescent mountain—it is this which is Lebanon's glory. And it is not European civilization and the march of liberty and the diffusion of refinement and learning, nor is it the incidental benefits resulting from his advent which brings the brightest lustre to the name of Jesus. But it is his Spirit embodied—his hidden life again appearing in some beneficent, resolute, lofty believer—it is the Christlike Christian who is the glory of Christ.

The first thing that strikes us in the cedar is the firmness of its root. It is not content to drop a few slack fibres into the yielding loam; but it thrusts its sturdy wedge into the cloven rock, and pushes far below the brushwood in search of stronger moorings; and so, when the tempest comes down, it

* Rev. i. 14.

springs elastic to the hurricanes on its buttress of subterraneous boughs, and amid all the veerings of the blast, finds gallant purchase in its network of cables. The cedar has a root. The Christian has faith. He knows whom to believe, and he knows that he believes him. He is well persuaded that Jesus is the Son of God, and the Saviour of sinners. He is fully assured that Christ's blood cleanseth from all sin, and has efficacy enough to cleanse his own. He knows that Christ offers to be a Saviour to him, and he thankfully consents that he shall. And as his mind is made up on the sin-atoning efficacy and God-glorifying tendency of the decease accomplished at Jerusalem, he is equally persuaded of the surpassing loveliness and peerless claims of Immanuel himself. He has discovered so much of grace and truth, so much of Divine glory and transforming goodness in the Beloved of the Father, and is so affected by finding that this Saviour is willing to be his guide through life, and his portion in eternity, that his choice is fixed and his heart is won. For him to live will be Christ. And so, brethren, the beginning of all blessedness is to possess clear views, and a conclusive faith. Some deprecate distinct ideas. They prefer music without words—the goodly sound of the Gospel without its significance. And if they have faith, it is faith in confusion—faith without solid foundation. If they be cedars, they are cedars planted in mud—cedars in the sand. The cedars of Lebanon are rooted in the turfy sod, and riveted in the mountain rock. Know what to believe, and why. Read and hear and think and pray till your realizations be vivid, and your convictions sure and steadfast. Never rest till you know beyond all controversy, if you do not know it already, that the Bible is God's book—nor till you exactly understand and can easily state the one way of salvation. Never rest till you be able to intrust your everlasting interests to Jesus Christ, nor till you have some clear evidence that you are born again, and so made meet for the kingdom of heaven. Never rest till you know that your Redeemer liveth, nor till you feel that because he liveth you shall live also. "Your case will be very trying if ever called to part with all for Christ, and not sure of him either." And your departure from time will be dismal, if it be only the force of sickness that drives you away, and not the face of Jesus that draws you—if you see plainly the grisly hand and the leveled shaft of the destroyer to fly from, but not the open arms and smiling embrace of the Saviour to leap into.

The cedar is a thirsty tree. It is distinguished from many of its kindred by its avarice of water. We once saw two of them at Chelsea, which were said to have grown rapidly for a hundred years, till two ponds in the garden were filled with rubbish—after which they grew no more. And we remembered the words of Ezekiel, "Behold, the Assyrian was a cedar in Lebanon, with fair branches, and a shadowing shroud. The waters made him great, the deep set him up on high. His boughs were multiplied, and his branches became long, because of the multitude of waters. All the fowls of heaven made their nests in his boughs, and under his branches did the beasts of the field bring forth their young, and under his shadow dwelt great nations. Thus fair was his grandeur, for his root was by great waters. The cedars in the garden of God could not hide him, the fir trees were not like him, all the trees of Eden envied him."* And so there are Christians planted by the rivers—believers of stately growth and luxuriant shadow—so tall that, even in the garden of God, and among the cedars, they cannot be hid. For clear eyed, time-penetrating faith, such an overtopping saint was Abraham, who athwart the expanse of nineteen centuries could see Christ's day, and exult with a disciple's joy. For prompt gratitude and ecstatic adoration, such an exalted saint was David, whose "glorying" slept so lightly that the softest touch awoke it,† and whose palpitating psaltery was so accustomed to Hallelujahs, that sorrow struck them out as readily as joy, and, oft as he changed the chords the loyal harp, would only sing the praises of Jehovah. For high-hearted devotion to his God, such an elevated saint

* Ezek. xxxi. 3—9. † Psa. lvii. 8.

was Daniel, whose lofty statesmanship, and spotless career, and lovely bearing to his brethren, were but the various expressions of the self-same thing, to which he owed his miraculous escapes and his frequent revelations; "O man greatly beloved, thy prayer is heard." And for burning love to Jesus Christ, self-forgetful, self-consuming, such a pre-eminent saint was Paul, to whom the beloved image of his Master shone in every type and shadow of the old economy, who could trace the myrrh-dropping fingers on the tongs and snuffers of the tabernacle; who could hear the voice of Jesus through the roar of the Adriatic, and lean upon his arm before Nero's judgment-seat; to whom the affliction in which Christ came was more welcome than an angel visitor, and as the summons to Christ's presence, death itself the object of desire. Such noble and commanding characters have there been, that none could hide them, and none were like them, and under the awe or the attraction of their goodness, good men wished to resemble them. "The trees of Eden envied them." It is not only Secretary Cecil who could have changed the palace for the preacher's cottage, rightly declaring, "There dwells as much happiness as can be known on earth;" but men of God have been provoked to press forward by the higher attainments of their brethren. "In one I have been animated by ardent activity for the glory of Christ, and the salvation of souls. In another I was pleased and softened by conspicuous meekness and gentleness of spirit. In a third, I was excited to love and good works by the fervent charity and brotherly kindness I beheld; and in a fourth, I was led to abase myself, and confess the pride of my heart, from the humility and brokenness of spirit which struck me." But when you come to look closely into the matter, and inquire to what secret cause these lofty cedars owe their growth; whence is it that their influential and impressive characters have derived their admirable grace, you always find that communion with God is the comprehensive source of their pre-eminent piety. They are abundant in religious exercises. They are mighty in the Scriptures. They are men of prayer. They are frequenters of the sanctuary. They are lovers of Christian fellowship. They are delighted observers of the Sabbath. But, after all, ordinances are to them but avenues or audience chambers. It is a Bible in which God speaks, a closet in which God hearkens, a sanctuary in which God's countenance shines, which they desire of the Lord, and seek to attain. And finding these, they find the living God himself. Their fellowship is with the Father and the Son. They grow into the knowledge of the Divine perfections. They grow in reverence, and trust, and love. They grow in perceptions of their own infinite vileness, and consequently in appreciation of the blood which pardons, and the Spirit who cleanses. They grow in self-distrust, and in dependence on God. They grow in self-condemnation, and in longings for that world where they will sin no more. And whilst they are solidly growing in these inward experiences, they have, unawares to themselves, expanded the long branches, and shadowing shroud of a great cedar. They have become the admiration and resort of others. The affections of many nestle in their boughs, and under their shadow dwell those who seek to profit by their counsel and their company. And just as there is growth in the multitude of waters, so there is decrepitude and decay where the waters fail. Like the Chelsea cedars, you will meet with professors who, for many years together, have not grown an inch. The rubbish of secularity or idleness has filled up the two pools of Bible reading and secret prayer; and a form of godliness, and a few evangelical phrases still remembered; a stunted top, and a bundle of scrubby branches, are all that remains a memorial of their better days.

Another thing notable in the cedar is the vigour of its goodly boughs. Some trees, especially trees of the forest, growing in groups, have fragile boughs, and cannot abide in bleak and windy places. But the cedar is not more remarkable for the depth of its roots than for the strength of its branches. Not grafted on nor jointed in, but the brawny limbs deep rooted in the massy bole, presenting a broad surface to the sun, and a thin edge to the tempest, too elastic to snap, and too sturdily set in their socket to flutter in the breeze, these boughs are the very emblem of graceful strength and vigorous majesty. The Christian is a man of faith, and therefore a man of principle. His creed is principle. His practice is the same. Roots and branches make one tree; and faith and practice make one Christian. And those are the noblest and most serviceable Christians whose convictions are so firm, and whose characters are so strong, that nothing can affright them from their faith, and nothing deter them from their duty. In this respect, that father of the Church was a goodly cedar, who, when nearly the whole of Christendom had yielded to the God-denying heresy, lifted up in banishment his solitary voice, proclaiming the Saviour's Deity, "*Athanasius against the world!*" And they were goodly cedars, those Waldensian worthies, who, amid the rocks and snows of Piedmont, through five-and-thirty persecutions, held fast the faith of Jesus, and though gashed by the Savoyard spear, and scorched by the Romish faggot, carried down from earliest time to the present hour Christ's pure Gospel. And he was a goodly cedar, that Knox, who never feared the face of man. The fire of surrounding martyrdoms but warmed his roots, and gave a rush of quicker zeal to his fervent spirit; and whilst the axe of tyrants threatened, he firmly stood his ground till the idols fell, and the evangel flourished, and Scotland was free

And so was that Saxon Luther, whom the Emperor and his legions tried to terrify, but in the strength of God he came on them so mighty, that men and devils were dismayed, —that Luther whom the Pope's emissary tried to bribe, but was obliged to write back to his master, "This German beast has no regard for gold." And so were those goodly cedars, Huss, and Jerome, and Ridley, and Patrick Hamilton, and many more, who counted their lives not dear that they might keep the testimony of Jesus; and amidst flames and torture finished their joyful course —goodly cedars, which burning were not consumed. And not to multiply instances of confessor courage and martyr-heroism, it is the self-same holy energy and decision of Christian character, which have developed in self-denying services and costly sacrifices. Francke devoting all his time and all his fortune to his Orphan Hospital;—Vanderkemp, labouring as a brickmaker that he might be better fitted for his mission to the Hottentots; —the "Apostle of the Indians," wringing the rain water from his clothes, and lying all night in the forest with nothing but a tree to shelter him;—Richard Baxter, refusing a bishopric; John Wesley, preferring active labour to the preparation of a pamphlet in his own defence, "Brother, when I devoted to God my ease, my time, my life, did I except my reputation?"—those in whom Christian principle has been so strong, that at its bidding they have abandoned lucrative situations and tempting prospects, that they might keep holy the Sabbath, that they might preserve inviolate honesty, truthfulness, and integrity, that they might maintain a conscience void of offence; all these have put forth in their day the strength of the goodly cedar.

The cedar "grows" from year to year. The solid timber of its trunk grows denser, and more compact, and new layers are added to its girth, so that when it is eventually felled, you can almost say, by counting the concentric rings, how many summers it has seen. A living Christian grows. His character confirms. Duties, which when first performed were a crucifixion of the flesh, and a triumph of faith, become easy and familiar habits. Promises, the fulfilment of which he at first credited on the mere authority of God, have now received the yea and amen of a long experience. In the homely words of Robert Bruce, "When I was young the Lord compelled me to live by faith, but now he feeds his old servant with great morsels of sense." Religion has become his better and more beauteous nature. He is past the danger of being ashamed of Christ. The awkwardness and fear of man which made him once so fond of obscurity, and so afraid of the Jews, have passed away, and he is no longer averse to be ranked among the peculiar people, and regarded as a disciple of Jesus. There are apologies which he has ceased to make, and difficulties which he has ceased to feel. The lions of his youth have disappeared from the street, and the grasshopper, which was a burden to his early faith, is no disturbance to his maturer piety. There are sins which no longer beset him, and fears which no longer distress him. He has outgrown the spirit of speculation and controversy, and in meek docility, sits down at the Master's feet, listening to—"Thus saith the Lord." He has lost the desire for theological novelties and religious curiosities, and is only anxious for such new things as come out of the old Bible treasury. He has outlived the dogmatism and harsh judging of his sanguine prime, and no longer calls for fire from heaven on the Samaritans. He has left behind him the vanity which gave an air of flippancy and self-conceit to his earlier efforts, and raised a prejudice against himself, if not a distaste at religion. And, perhaps, he has outlived the fear of dying. At one time there was something ghastly in the look of the last enemy: but now, looking unto Jesus, he has learned to look beyond it. "There is something in the heart of Christ, and something in my own, which will not be at rest till I be set down upon Mount Zion. My eyes are turning gladly towards death, as the only sure period of his absence, and of these agonies of separation." *

Brethren, would you know whether you are growing in grace—improving and advancing in personal Christianity? Then tell

* Letters of Dr. John Love.

us, Is your faith more firm? Have the truths to which you once consented strengthened into settled convictions? Have they become first principles, and do they instinctively prompt you to corresponding action? Is your piety more pervasive? Does it decide your conduct, and give the casting vote in doubtful conjunctures of your history? "Does it regulate your daily demeanour as a husband, wife, parent, child, master, servant? Does it come abroad with you, out of your closets into your houses, your shops, your fields? Does it journey with you, and buy and sell for you?" Does it stand at your elbow, and keep watch at the door of your lips? Is your heart larger? Instead of looking merely on your own things, have you learned to look on the things of others? Do you love the brotherhood? And however much you may prize your own denomination, do you rejoice to hear that godliness revives and religion spreads in other communions? Have you a public spirit?—a missionary spirit?—a spirit of zeal? In the efforts made to protect the Sabbath,—to rescue missionary stations from Romish intrigue and warlike rapacity;—in the efforts to educate the ignorant, and reclaim the vicious, and ameliorate the condition of the working classes, do your whole souls accord? Have these present objects of philanthropy your suffrage, your sympathy, your prayers? But, above all, does your love to the Lord Jesus grow? Whether it be in this world or another that you first expect to see him as he is, do you desire the sight? Do you distinctly feel that the same Saviour who was such a disappointment to the Pharisees, and who, after he had been so long time with them, was so little known by Philip and Thomas and the rest—are you sure that he is just the Saviour whom you desire, the very one whose presence will make, in any place, your heaven? Have you beheld his glory, full of grace and truth; and has that glory so inflamed your spirit that, like the ship to its haven, like the needle to its magnet, like the dove to its window, your soul will only reach its final rest when it comes home to Him to depart no more?

The Maronites ascribe a singular faculty to the cedar. They say that on the approach of snowy weather, it bends its branches upwards, so as to receive the falling flakes on the sides of a slender pyramid.* Prepared for the tempest, it only looks more graceful under it, and the storm which could not rend its boughs, soon melts in irrigation round its roots. And though the cedar's power to predict the tempest may exist only in the imagination of these sons of the mountain, the les-

* A French traveller of last century relates this, and apparently believes it. The cedar does not retain its self protecting instinct in this country. There was a noble specimen in the Royal Gardens at Kew, on which, a few winters ago, the snow lay so heavy, that one windy night its great branches fractured, with a report so loud that the villagers mistook it for the firing of guns.

son is to us not the less instructive. It is in a way somewhat similar that the Lord prepares his people for trial. Sometimes they have a presentiment of approaching calamity, and are led to cry, "Be not far from me, for trouble is near."* But often, and still more mercifully, the coming evil is hid, and all their preparation is unwonted heavenly-mindedness. Like the cedar lifting up its boughs, they lift up their hearts, and know not that it is their Lord putting them in an attitude to bear the storm. They feel a joy unspeakable to-day, and find the explanation in the grief of the morrow. But still the joy of the Lord has strengthened them, the self-devotion and ascending affections of these preparatory moments, have put them in the posture on which the tempest comes down most lightly. "On Easter Sunday, 1824," writes one, "I rose before six in the morning, earlier than I had been able to do for a month before, on account of indisposition. I kneeled down a minute or two after I had risen, and completely resigned myself to God, giving myself up to him in a way which I had never been able to do before. I rose from my knees with a sacred feeling that I was not my own, being 'bought with a price,' but the actual property of another, who I was perfectly willing should do what he pleased with his own. I had a peculiarly calm and composed state of mind all the day. In the evening I coughed twice, and broke

* Psalm xxii. 11.

a blood vessel."* And this was the beginning of the illness from which she never finally recovered, but during which, divine consolations never forsook her. In the Journal of Mrs. Fletcher, one entry closes, "Certainly I have now scarce any cross. Thou hast made my cup to run over. Yea, thou hast made me to forget all my sorrows. There is not a comfort I can wish for, which I have not; but, Lord, I want more grace." The next begins, "When I wrote last, I was arrived at the summit of human felicity. But, O! how shall I write it!—On the 14th of August, the dreadful moment came. The sun of my earthly joys forever set, and the cloud arose which casts the sable on all my future life. At half-past ten that Sabbath night, I closed the eyes of my beloved." But from another passage it appears that just before the attack which ended his earthly labours, Mr. Fletcher and herself had been led to a very express devotement of themselves to God; and the consequence was, that her startled spirit soon found its quiet rest again. A thankful sense of her mercies made one pang the less in losing them; and the self-dedication in which she had joined, prepared her for the elevated and beneficent life worthy of one who had found a Husband in her Maker. And as the Lord secretly prepares his people for trial, so he supports them under it. Like the snow

* Memorials of Two Sisters.

which shapes the cedar into a new and graceful figure, sorrow gives the Christian a new aspect of loveliness. It brings out the meekness, the endurance, and elasticity of the better nature within him; and evinces how invulnerable is his hidden life. It was the cheerful remark of Mr. Wilberforce, when his wealth took wing, "I know not why my life is spared so long, except it be to show that a man can be as happy without a fortune as with one." Dr. Arnold had a sister, who, during twenty years of sickness, made it a rule never once to allude to her sufferings; and there have been many of God's servants, whom his Spirit has so mightily strengthened, that it was a great sight, it was treading ground which God's presence made holy, when called to witness their patient endurance and joyful constancy. And like the cedar, ready for trial, and supported under it, the believer is the better for it when it has passed away. What is spring but winter melted? What is the sap which now gushes vital in these branches, but the snow which lately covered them with its frosty load? And what is vigorous piety, but temptation vanquished? What is experience, but tribulation thawed by patience? And what is heaven itself, but light affliction transformed to exceeding glory?*

We might mention other properties of the cedar. Like the palm, it is evergreen.

* Rom. v. 3, 4. 2 Cor. iv. 17.

Though a native of the mountains, and used to wintry weather, it never sheds its leaves. And these leaves, as well as its bark and wood, are aromatic. Even when the snow is loading its branches, the cedar is fragrant; but it is in those blessed and vernal days when snows are melting, when the April sun is lavishing his light and heat to the balmy air, and the whole life of the mountain is gushing through the opening flowers and carolling birds and leaping lambs—it is then that in the bursting of fresh foliage and in the flow of beaded gums, the cedar loads the air with incense, and flings afar "the smell of Lebanon." And so a gracious soul is ever fresh, ever vital, ever green. But there are times when the winter is past, and the Sun of Righteousness shines, the April season of the soul; times when a whole tide of happy life flows into the dilating spirit, and the joy of Jesus circulates expansive and reviving through every opening faculty, and enlarging grace. And it is then—then, when every twig of the cedar is tufted with new softness and beauty, and when the nestling birds are singing in the branches—it is then, when the love of the Spirit circulates anew, and the soul exults in God its Saviour; it is then that it is good to be near the happy and fresh-filled believer. In such society, and at such a season, the atmosphere is odour. The south wind wakes, and the spices flow. Heaven has opened, and the winter fled. God smiles, and the soul expands. The

Holy Spirit stirs within, and verdure mantles to the topmost bough. And in the wafted gladness and delicious air, every alert disciple feels it is surely good to be here.

We might have added, the cedar is sound to the last; and the believer perseveres to the end, "to show that the Lord is upright; he is a rock, and there is no unrighteousness with him." But we only mention one particular farther. The palm is most productive at the last. It brings forth in old age its largest, richest fruit. The cedar is most useful when dead. It is most productive when its place knows it no more. There is no timber like it. Firm in the grain, and capable of the finest polish, the tooth of no insect will touch it, and time himself can hardly destroy it. Diffusing a perpetual fragrance through the chambers which it ceils, the worm will not corrode the book which it protects, nor the moth corrupt the garment which it guards. All but immortal itself, it transfuses its amaranthine qualities to the objects around it; and however stately in the forest, or brave on the mountain's brow, it is more serviceable in Solomon's palace, and more sanctified when set up as pillars in the Temple, and carved into door-posts and lintels for the House of the Lord. Every Christian is useful in his life, but the goodly cedars are most useful afterwards. Joseph, while he lived, saved much people alive, and his own lofty goodness was an impressive and elevating pattern to his relenting and admiring brethren. But as an instance of special providence, and an example of untarnished excellence amidst terrible temptations, Joseph dead has spoken to more than Joseph living. The sweet singer of Israel, while he lived, taught many to handle the harp, and infected not a few with his thankful, adoring spirit. But David being dead, yet singeth; and you can hardly name the psalm, or hymn, or spiritual song, of which the lesson was not learnt from the son of Jesse. Paul, in his living day, preached many a sermon, and made many a convert to the faith of Jesus. But Paul being dead, yet preacheth, and they were sermons from his sepulchre which converted Luther, and Zuingle, and most of our modern evangelists. And Luther is dead, but the Reformation lives. Calvin is dead, but his vindication of God's free and sovereign grace will never die. Knox, Melville, and Henderson are dead, but Scotland still retains a Sabbath and a Christian peasantry, a Bible in every house, and a school in every parish. Bunyan is dead, but his bright spirit still walks the earth in its "Pilgrim's Progress." Baxter is dead, but souls are still quickened by the "Saint's Rest," and the "Call to the Unconverted." Cowper is dead, but the "golden apples" are still as fresh as when newly gathered in the "silver basket" of the Olney Hymns. Eliot is dead, but the missionary enterprise is young. Henry Martyn is dead, but who can count the apostolic spirits, who, phœnix-wise, have started from his funeral pile? Howard is dead, but modern philanthropy is only commencing its career. Raikes is dead, but the Sabbath-schools go on. Wilberforce is dead, but the negro will find for ages, a protector in his memory.

And though you, Christian brother, may not occupy a place of prominence, you may fill a place of usefulness. If not a cedar of the mountain, you may be a cedar of the vale. Seek a clear understanding of scriptural truth. Be fully persuaded in your mind. See to it that a living Saviour be indeed the sun of your affections and the centre of your desires. Cultivate a strenuous piety. Alike combat intellectual laziness and spiritual lethargy. Be ready for every good work. Be ready to give a reason for the hope that is in you. And pray that the Lord would maintain you ever ready for his providential will. Instead of yielding to every passing influence, seek a character so consistent, so meekly resolute, so cheerfully devout, that sin will find no sanction in your silence, and irreligion no excuse in your gloom. And more especially among familiar friends and in your house at home, strive to walk wisely in a perfect way. Begin and end the day with God. Let salt season your speech, and let Christian elevation pervade your demeanour. Let the peace of God rule in your heart, and let its power at once to strengthen and soften be seen in that majestic principle with which worldliness dares not to tamper, and that continual benignity which makes even worldliness wistful. And thus, when you yourself "grow" here no longer, even the irreligious will think of something very lofty and lovely when they think of you.

THE PALM

BY

THE REV. JAMES HAMILTON,

MINISTER OF THE FREE CHURCH, REGENT SQUARE,
LONDON.

"The Righteous shall flourish like the Palm tree."—
PSALMS xcii. 12.

PHILADELPHIA:
PRESBYTERIAN BOARD OF PUBLICATION

THE PALM.

Dear Reader,—You have named the name of Jesus. You have been led to avow yourself the Saviour's disciple. And, if sincere and intelligent in your profession, you are very different from the multitude, and from what you yourself once were. To you Christ is now a real person. You are persuaded that he is the Son of God and the Saviour of sinners. You believe that 1800 years ago, he poured out his precious blood on a cross at Jerusalem, as an atonement for sin, and by his obedience to death brought in everlasting righteousness. You are assured that he is now at the Father's right hand, a Prince and a Saviour, bestowing repentance and the remission of sins. Your own hope is in Christ. You know not another name to which you can trust your eternal interests, but Christ Jesus you can and do rely on. And since you ascertained Christ's ability and willingness to save, there has been a change in your affections and hopes, your

12

principles and habits. Your temperament may be cold; nevertheless, by you Christ is loved and adored. Your faith may be feeble and your prospects confused; still you have learned to recognize a Friend in Immanuel and a home in heaven. Your motives may be mixed and unstable; still your obedience is new, and you often find a holy impulse, a filial instinct, the joy or the love of Christ constraining you. Your character may be very defective; but still you can perceive that it is altered—for now you love to pray and read the Bible. You are happy among the excellent of the earth. The meditation of God is sweet, the day of God is welcome, and the house of God is dear. If a Christian at all, your case will be another fulfilment of the universal rule, "If any man be in Christ, he is a new creature."

But along with the hope of sincerity, you may have a painful sense of deficiency. You feel that you are neither so happy nor so holy as a Christian might be. You would like to reach a character more explicit, a faith more firm, and an experience more vivid than are sought by ambiguous and commonplace professors. You perceive that it is a high mark which the Gospel sets before you, and that the consistent Christian is not only a new but a noble creature. But if such completeness and consistency of character be the objects of your desire, you should make them the subject of earnest thought and prayerful effort. With the Bible for a directory, and the Holy Spirit for a teacher, there is nothing august and nothing amiable in vital Christianity which you may not long and hope to see developed in yourself. The Father is glorified when disciples are fruitful. The Church is strong, when its members are mutual supports and incitements; and the Gospel spreads when living epistles commend it. Selecting as mottoes two scriptural emblems, the palm and the cedar—the one representing personal religion in its gracefulness, the other piety in its grandeur; the one, the beauty of true holiness—the other, its majesty: and both together the blessedness of its possessor, and the benefits which he confers on others—we humbly and affectionately offer to our brethren the hints which have been suggested to ourselves.

There is something instructive in the very place where the palm tree grows. It is not in the sheltered depths of the forest, nor with its roots struck deep in the fertile loam. It grows in the desert. All round the ridgy sand is burning, and often its pillar of verdure springs direct from the scorching dust. And it is in the desert that trees of righteousness grow. This earth is a land of emptiness. Its mould is not the soil from which you would expect aught spiritual or holy to spring. And when in a world like this—a world so sensual and depraved, and so embittered against the living God—when in such a world you alight on a man of blameless life, and devout disposition, and heavenly aspirations, it is the same surprise as encountering the bright and laden palm on the dusty edge of the desert. You may feel that your own abode is not the favourable place for cultivating personal piety. Your abode is not a cottage imbedded in the calm of rural Sabbaths, and, by the soft voice of silent monitors, inviting you, Eden-wise, to communion with God. Your lot is not cast under the protective shadow of a domestic sanctuary, or amid the innocent safeguards and virtuous inspiration of a hallowed and godly home. You live in a city where the dust of business is drifting all the week, and the din of occupation disturbs the day of rest. You are planted in a lonely lodging, or a prayerless household. And if your soul is to thrive at all, it must learn to "flourish" among strangers and scoffers. You must be a man of principle in the midst of profligacy, and a man of faith while surrounded with infidelity. "Thou, God, seest me!" must be inscribed in the dingy counting-room, and must move before you in letters of endearing light through the glare of the gas-lit mart. You must carry Bible rules into scenes of trickery and tumult, and must not suffer cunning men to beguile you of your simplicity, or knavish men to rob you of your equanimity. You must learn to be holy and harmless though in daily contact with duplicity, and must strive to lead Enoch's life: for, were Enoch living now, he would walk with God in the streets of London.

Though the palm starts bolt up from the burning sand, the sand is not its sustenance. The dust may have swept hot and stifling round its stem ;—but clear that dust away. The sand grows humid as you dig, and, by the time you reach the white fibres of the tap, the veins of water flow. And as, by and by, you gaze on the fringy rootlets floating in the well, you discern the secret of its joyous growth. No matter that the sky is brass and the desert dust, when crystal life is throbbing plentiful below. Doubtless this is a dry and thirsty land; but it is the land where ever and anon the eye is gladdened by some goodly palm. In strange and unexpected places you meet with fresh and lofty Christians. You wonder how they thrive. They do not grow as the lily ; for the lily is found in green pastures, and they do not belong to a lifesome communion. Nor do they spring as the willow ; for it springs by the water-courses, and they have not the benefit of the purest ordinances and the most refreshful ministrations. They are trees of the desert, like Enoch among the giant sinners of an early world; like Joseph among the wizards and beast-worshippers of Egypt; like Daniel in voluptuous Babylon; like David Brainerd among Indian savages; like Henry Martyn in stony-hearted Persia. Their life is hid. So pure amidst depravity, so loyal to God amidst idolatry, so devout and fervent amidst atheism and blasphemy, their heavenly-mindedness is a miracle. But beneath the dusty surface of this godless world, there is a well of water springing up to everlasting life. There is no spot so barren, and no soil so burning, no situation so adverse, but faith can find the Holy Spirit there. It needs only faith's penetrating root descending beneath the things which do appear,* to fetch up spiritual refreshment and invigoration where others pine and die. From a secret source the believer in Jesus draws his life. The morning portion of the word, the morning prayer, the morning meditation; these are the "stolen waters" which keep him green all day; and even in the desert there is a dew which, descending on his branches over night, brings him forth fragrant and lively to the morrow. You, my friends, who lead lives of secularity or drudgery, you who are often sighing—"Lord, what a wretched land is this;" remember that it is the land of the Bible, the land of prayer, the land of the promises, and, above all, the land of the Comforter's presence and power. To say nothing of periodic rains and weekly showers, the affluent irrigation of sanctified Sabbaths and communion feasts—a daily text and daily prayer, with the whole heart in them, would make you flourish like the palm. You would realize something of the life of God in your own soul, and your shining healthful aspect would awake the exclama-

* Heb. xi. 1.

tion, " O Lord of Hosts, blessed is the man whose strength is in thee."*

The palm is a tree of remarkable beauty. Apart from all its associations there is something in its slim uprightness, its verdant canopy, and the silvery flashes of its waving plumes which glads the eye that gazes. And so is there in a person truly gracious. If your character be completely Christian, if there be in it so much of grace that the gracious has all grown natural, if your affections be brought obedient to Christ Jesus, if your maxims of conduct be scriptural, and your motives in acting be Christian, there will be instruction and joy in beholding you. Your growth will be erect and aspiring. The ivy creeps and the bramble trails, but the palm, in its perpendicular uprightness, dwells on high, and seeks the things above. And the fairest Christians are those whose pure and lofty affections lift them sublimely above all that is low and debasing, and whose heaven-pointing demeanour betokens an upgoing heart. Whosoever is anxious to become a consistent and conspicuous Christian, must keep aloof from the mean enjoyments and paltry expedients, the tattling curiosity and malignant constructions, of a world incredulous of the highest goodness, because incapable of exerting it; and, aware that no permanent motive to well-doing can be found here below, he must seek it in that Saviour

* Psalm lxxxiv. 5.

whose smile it elicits, and in that heaven where it all will be found again. Some trees are crooked, but the palm is straight, and, standing forth in its unbending altitude, spreads all its foliage to the sun. And, if yours be a flourishing Christianity, there will be no crooks nor zigzags in it. A conscience void of offence will give a gay security to your goings out and comings in. Never meeting the neighbour whom you have injured, nor the man who has aught ignominious to allege against you; haunted by no sense of hollowness, and no forebodings for the future; harbouring no bitter feelings, and hiding no sinister designs, you will readily come to the light, and never fear that it will make your deeds too manifest. And just as your frank explicit character will declare you a child of day, your evenly sense and the sweetness of your disposition, will justify you as one of Wisdom's children. There are trees which have knots of weakness in their substance, and gnarled projections on their surface. But the palm is not only erect and tall; its stem is fair and even. From the root to the topmost tuft, it springs round, elegant, and equal, with neither galls nor disfiguring bunches. There are crotchetty Christians; but they are not palms. There are professors so peculiar that you can never count on them; what they are to-day is no presumption for what they shall be to-morrow. They may have many good points and noble qualities; but their fellowship is marred, and their usefulness frustrated, by whims which no sagacity can predict, and caprices to which not even "the patience of the saints" can conform. Do you, brethren, cultivate a meek and quiet spirit; that magnanimity which is calm and considerate, and which tries to look at this day's grievances in to-morrow's light; that elastic and happy temper which, being the growth of grace, shall be independent of the weather—that serenity which, whether in fog, or sickness, or hunger, or in sunshine, and health, and bodily comfort, "is not easily provoked;" that "charity which suffereth long and is kind, which hopeth all things, endureth all things." And if this grace be in you—if your spirit be so ruled that men find you the same yesterday and to-day—your heart fixed amidst vexations, and amidst all its trials your temper tranquil, they will perceive that the religion from above is full of good fruits, and will admire its peaceful fruits in you.

Nor must we forget that foliage which is one chief glory of the palm. Each several frond in its graceful arching, and its long and taper leaflets, with the gloss of unfading verdure, is such a natural symbol of hope and joy, and exultation, that the palm branch has stood for ages the emblem of victory. It was twisted into the verdant booths at the Feast of Tabernacles; it was borne aloft by the multitude when they escorted Messiah to his coronation in Jerusalem. "And lo! before the throne in heaven, and before the

Lamb, a great multitude, clothed with white robes, and palms in their hands." * And every believer should flourish like the palm. Not only should "his leaf never fade," † it should not even sully. Some leaves are so viscid and clammy, that the dust settles and adheres. And some professors, who perhaps are genuine, are so powdered over with a constant secularity that their leaf is always dingy. They are wayfaring trees; and if the shower of some special ordinance or solemnizing dispensation should wash their foliage into a momentary freshness, the cares of this life soon deface it again. But in the heart of the desert the palm contrives to cast the dust quick as it alights, and keeps its slender leaflets pure. And so, Christian brethren, be it your endeavour to maintain not only a blameless, but a beauteous character, the full circulation and the fresh attire of a flourishing Christianity. You must go into the world to-morrow. You must do many dull and irksome things, or many things apparently remote from religion. But if you have found out the secret of spiritual-mindedness, you will come home fit for the prayer meeting, or for the Christian friend, or the family worship. In the midst of all the secularities which have been floating around, you will keep your garments clean. The palm has no holiday clothing. Its branch is equally green, whether an emperor or an

* Rev vii. 9. † Psalm i. 3.

outlaw pass under it. Summer and winter it is always the same. And so a beauteous Christianity is that which loses none of its loveliness to the eye that oftenest views it. If you be respectable in public—if you be serious and fervent in the sanctuary—if your conversation be rational or religious in society—but if you be commonplace at home—if you be cross and censorious, frivolous and silly, worldly and wearisome at your own fireside—if you be one of those trees which need brushing before they are fit to be seen, such dusty affinities prove that your nature is not that of the palm. If full of sap, your leaf will be evergreen; and those who know you best will love you most, and be the best persuaded of your simplicity and godly sincerity. And to crown the whole; if yours be a palmy growth, yours will be a religion of happiness and praise. A fair sight it is when the breeze flits by, and every ray of the feathery coronet twinkles to the morning sun—the desert's anthem—the palm tree's orison. Nature gave the hint to man, and to God's glory waved her verdant plumes before the victor learned to wave them to his own. And so, dear friend, if yours be the right religion, it will be imbued with blessedness and clothed with praise. You "will be fat and flourishing," "to show that the Lord is upright." Through the greatness of his work your heart will be made right glad. His greatest work redemption, will often swell in upon your spirit with new surprise, and the Christ that is yours, and the Comforter that is yours, and the heaven which is soon to be yours, will bear back your waking glory into astonished silence and heart-murmured adoration; and lesser gifts, less, but most precious, will be a sweet relief to the overmastering emotion; and, by giving outlet to the gratitude, you will sanctify the gift, and seal it in sacredness and sweet memorial on your own soul. Habitual faith will give perennial cheerfulness. If "fat" you will be "flourishing." The peace of God within will force off the withered twigs of care and foreboding and worldly-mindedness, and give you the daily freshness of one careful for nothing. "I am now," writes one, "near the end of my warfare. I never had such a variety of affairs to manage as a man in so much business as yourself, but I had a large young family very dear to me, and not enough for their maintenance from year to year; and, in case of my death, they were to be destitute. I was, however, wonderfully free and cheerful in my heart. I think I should not have been more so, if I had been without a child. My preservative was wholly this: 'He that hath the Son hath life.' A full and powerful conviction of this truth was attended with constant prayer for them and myself, that we might have this one thing needful, which by this means grew in price and value. Was Christ enough for peace, comfort, and joy to the first Christians; and is He not now the same? Will he not be enough for me and my children?" And to like purport writes another: "Yesterday I was much taken up in house affairs. Various things occurred which would at some times have been a burden, but every thing seemed blest. These words were all day the language of my heart:—

"With thee conversing I forget
All time, and toil, and care;
Labour is rest, and toil is sweet,
If thou, my God, be there."

Few trees can equal the palm in absolute usefulness. Its shadow refreshes the weary traveller. Its sweet and abundant fruit restores his strength. And when his soul faileth him for thirst, its welcome telegraph announces, Here is water. The light-house of the wilderness, nature's simple hostelry, its beacon has darted life into many a glassy eye, and has forwarded to his home, which he hardly hoped to see again, many a sinking wanderer;—so that glad associations and grateful offices have gone far to enhance its beauty. And in the tender mercy of God there are distributed through the Church of Christ, and consequently, through the world, many persons who, in beneficence, flourish like the palm. To do good and communicate they never forget. They cannot avoid it. It is now spontaneous with them, for God gave them the disposition when he gave them their new nature. Like a cool shadow in a scorching day, their counsel revives the perplexed, and their sympathy cheers the sad. Like the clustering dates ungrudgingly showered on the passenger, their generosity and hospitality are a boon to all who need them. And like the palm tree pointing to the hidden well, their sure direction guides the weary seeker to the Fountain where he drinks and lives forever. Such a one was Barnabas, the Son of Consolation, in whose large heart and tender wisdom, afflicted consciences and wounded spirits found the balm which healed them, "a good man, and full of the Holy Ghost." And such were Gaius, and Aquila, and Lydia, and Dorcas, whose willing roof and untiring bounty made churches their debtors, and who found in the prayers of the poor their payment. And such was Philip the Evangelist, who put the timely question to the Ethiopian, and business-like and brother-like sat down in the chariot beside him, and pointed out so plain that way to heaven which the earnest stranger was so fain to find. And such in later times have been many of the Church Universal's worthies: Bernard Gilpin, whose open hand and inviting door softened towards the Gospel the rude heart of Northumberland; John Thornton, of whom it was remarked, "Were there but a thousand loving Christians of great opulence likeminded with him, the nation would be convinced of the good operation of the Gospel;" William Wilberforce, who, in addition to countless acts of considerate philanthropy, sought out and sent to college young men of principle and promise, and saw his liberality rewarded when they became judges of the land, and distinguished ministers of the Gospel; Howell Harris, who filled his Trevecca mansion with scores of disabled and destitute Christians, and, amidst the tears of a hundred adopted children, passed away to that beloved Saviour whom hungry he fed, and a stranger he had taken in;* Mrs. Fletcher, of Madeley, who devoted her long widowhood to prayer and active kindness, and re-peopled her desolate home with orphans and the pious poor; John Newton, whose dusky Coleman-street chamber shone with a heavenly radiance in many a memory, for there, amid his affectionate explanations, the cross stood out to their tearful view, and for the first time they learned to find in a Saviour's side the double refuge from sin and from sorrow. And such in your place and your measure may each of you who are Christians at all aspire to become. "Herein is the Father glorified that ye bear much fruit." Kind looks, kind words, kind deeds, advice thoughtfully and honestly given, trouble cheerfully taken, visits to the sick and the mourning, when your heart goes with you and you are in a mood for prayer, gifts of your substance, large enough to make you interested in the cause to which you contribute, and intercessions as earnest as these gifts are cordial: such are true fruits of right-

* Matt. xxv. 35, 40.

eousness; such are the genuine produce of a thriving palm.

And not to enlarge too much, we merely notice the circumstance that this interesting tree is productive to the last, and brings forth its best fruit in old age. The best dates are said to be gathered when it has reached a hundred years. So is it with eminent Christians: the older the better; the older the more beautiful; nay, the older the more useful; and, different from worldlings, the older the happier. The best Christians are those who improve to the end, who grow in grace and in the knowledge of Jesus Christ to the very close of life. They loved him at first, but now they love him more. At first they were selfish, and only sought to escape from wrath; now they are jealous of the Saviour's honour, and long to be saved from sin. At first they only thought of the Priest; now they perceive the Priest upon a throne, and love not only the Saviour's cross, but the Saviour's yoke, and the Saviour's laws. One Jesus is their King. And they grow in knowledge of themselves. The truth to which they once assented becomes a deep-wrought experience. "In me, that is, in my flesh, dwelleth no good thing." And the discovery of this depravity, the knowledge how debased and worthless their nature has become, instead of making them morose and bitter towards their fellow-sharers in the fall, makes them lenient and considerate. They know themselves too well, to expect perfection in their friends, and find brethren to whom they can stick close in the face of obvious failings; and even when they hear of awful wickedness, indignation is chastened by shame and self-consciousness. It is something of the old Reformer's feeling when he saw the malefactor led to prison:—"There, but for the grace of God, goes John Bradford." And they grow in wisdom. Long experience, and still more the secret of the Lord, dispassionate observation and heavenly-mindedness, have given them sagacity; and sometimes in homely adages, sometimes in direct and sober counsel, they deal forth that mellow wisdom. And they grow in spirituality. We have seen those aged pilgrims to whom earthly things at last grew insipid; they had no curiosity for the news of the day, and little taste for fresh and entertaining books. They stuck to God's testimonies, and you never went in to see them but the ample Bible lay open on the table or the counterpane; and they could tell the portion which had been that morning's food, or the meditation of the previous night. The word of God dwelt in them so richly, that you could see they were becoming fit to dwell with God; for when a mind has become thoroughly scriptural, it wants but another step to make it celestial. And the last harvest came, and the last gleanings of their precious words, and when next we went that way, their place knew them no longer. They were flourishing in the courts of God's house on high, and we should a under their shadow and be regaled by their goodness no more. But when we recollected how fair their Christian profession was, how beneficent and serviceable they had ever been, and remembered that their last days were their brightest, and their last fruits their fairest, we said over to ourselves, "The righteous shall flourish like the palm tree. Those that be planted in the house of the Lord shall flourish in the courts of our God. They shall bring forth fruit in old age; they shall be fat and flourishing; to show that the Lord is upright; he is my Rock, and there is no unrighteousness with him."

Dear Christian reader, when your own ear cannot hear it, may this be your eulogy; when your own eye cannot read it, may this be your epitaph. In the meanwhile, for the sake of that Saviour who is dishonoured by proud and selfish and unlovely disciples, do you strive and pray for consistency. And for your own soul's sake, which is dulled by defective views, and depressed by each besetting sin, do you seek a serene and lofty faith, do you covet earnestly a blameless conversation. Let your triumphs over self, and your high-hearted zeal for the Saviour, let the largeness of your spirit and your heavenly elevation, let the exuberance of your goodness and the multitude of its special acts, let the fulness of your affections and the freshness of your feelings, and the abundance of your beneficence, make the Christian manifest and unmistakable. Let your happy piety be the far-eyed signal announcing an oasis in the desert, and pray that your church or congregation may become to weary pilgrims another Elim, where when they came they found "twelve wells of water, and threescore and ten palm trees."

When speaking of "the Vine," we tried to indicate the true source of religious vitality. "The Cedar" we took as an emblem of the Christian character in its strength; and "the Palm" as a type of its beauty. And though the sketch has been rapid, we fondly hope that in some reader it has awakened the desire to share this life, and to behold this fair and lofty character his own.

The main thing is to begin where God himself begins. At this moment you may feel yourself so vile, that you do not see how you can ever become holy. You perceive in the past such guilt, and in the present such sin and confusion, that you cannot imagine how you can ever commence a career of piety. But begin where God begins. His first announcement is peace and good will.* His aspect towards you is compassion and kindest entreaty. In Christ he is reconciling you to himself;† and in order to enjoy the instant friendship of the Most High, you have only

* Luke ii. 14. † 2 Cor. v. 19.

to exchange the frown of aversion or distrust for the smile of confidence and complacency. To see a propitious God, you have only to look up with a believing eye; and to receive his great gift of pardon, you have only to open an empty hand. This is God's method;* and if made divinely wise, you will reciprocate this method. You will avail yourself of that atonement which cancels the past, and you will receive that proffered righteousness, which, the moment it is yours, renders you as safe as if you were personally and absolutely innocent. There may be a dim devotion and an ascetic scrupulosity in which there is little of Gospel joy; but that piety is the healthiest and most prosperous, which from pardon accepted dates its distinct beginning, and which from the peace of God admitted, derives its serene and sunny strength. Therefore, if you are desirous of holiness, begin by accepting forgiveness.

It is in resorting to the Saviour direct and in receiving from his divine fulness, that spiritual life begins; and it is by communion that this life is sustained. As they sing in the Lutheran hymn, "I live where'er I love;"† — if Jesus be rightly loved, the thoughts will be much with him, and the life will be moulded by him. The secret of eminent piety lies here. The Apostle had

* Rom. iii. 22, 24–26; v. 18. 1 Cor. i. 30. 1 John v. 11

† "Ich lebe wo ich liebe."

fully attained it when he wrote, "I live, and yet I live not: it is Christ who lives in me."* And, dear reader, the more that the thought of the Lord Jesus mingles with your other thoughts; the more things that you try to do in his strength and name; the more exultingly that you realize your relation to him; and the more vehemently that his love constrains you, the more radiant will your character become, and the more of heaven will you carry with you through the world.

* Gal. ii. 20.

THE OLIVE

BY

THE REV. JAMES HAMILTON,

MINISTER OF THE FREE CHURCH, REGENT SQUARE,
LONDON.

"The Lord called thy name, A green olive tree, fair, and of goodly fruit."—JER. xi. 16.

PHILADELPHIA:
PRESBYTERIAN BOARD OF PUBLICATION.

THE OLIVE.

There are two kinds of olive trees to which reference is made in the word of God,—the wild, and the cultivated. In some respects, the one may be said to bear a close resemblance to the other, insomuch that a superficial observer, at an early period of the year, might not be able to discriminate between the two. Looking merely at the foliage, or the blossoms, or the branches, and forming his judgment accordingly, it would not, perhaps, be surprising if he came at once to the conclusion, that the one was by no means inferior to the other. But there is one point in which they are very different. The one is altogether sterile, or the fruit which it produces is entirely useless, if not positively deleterious. The other is productive of fruit,—fruit that is exceedingly valuable,—fruit that is capable of being applied to many useful purposes. And hence the importance of the test which the Bible furnishes,—"By their fruits ye shall know them."

By the same criterion we are to judge of the religious character of men. If they are Christians in deed and in truth, there must be fruit. But the fruit in every case may not be equally abundant. In some it may be thirty-fold; in others it may be sixty-fold; and in others still it may be an hundred-fold. For there are different degrees in the attainments of different Christians. They are not all of them precisely alike. In various respects they differ from each other. Nevertheless there is one point in which they all agree. They come to maturity; they bring forth fruit. That is the great test of Christian character; and unless we can stand that test, all our assumption of the Christian name, all our observance of religious ordinances, all our profession of attachment to the cause of Christ, will be of no avail. For it is not by men's professions, but by their fruits that we are to know them. By their fruits! Not by their position in the vineyard of God. They may be planted by the rivers of water, and fostered by the genial influences of heaven; and yet there may be no fruit. The tree itself may be corrupt. Not by the verdure of the foliage,—not by the luxuriance of the blossoms.

These may be fraught with the odour of a sweet fragrancy, and very beautiful to look upon; but the frost of a single night may nip them in the bud, and the violence of a single blast may scatter them to the winds of heaven; and when the gathering of the harvest comes, there may be no fruit. By their fruits ye shall know them, not by their appearances; the appearances may be very good; the promises may be very fair; and these, in due time, may be followed by the fruit. But we are not to judge by the appearances; we are to judge by the fruit. The fruit is the test of the goodness of the tree.

But is there any way by which the wild olive can be converted into the fruitful; or any process in the natural world which demonstrates the possibility of such a change? Most assuredly there is. And how? It is not by subjecting the wild olive to the pruning-knife of the husbandman; nor by transplanting it into a soil richly cultivated; nor by making the fertilizing influences of heaven to descend upon it. Its natural condition, or its essential qualities will never be materially altered by any appliances of that kind, however carefully observed, and however, long continued. And though the fruit may be rendered more abundant than before, it will still be the fruit of a corrupt tree. It is contrary to the laws of the physical world that it can be otherwise.

But if you take a branch, and cut it off

from the wild olive, and engraft it into a good olive tree,—a tree which is distinguished for its fatness, and which brings forth precious fruit, then what is the result? To adopt the significant language of the Bible, it is regenerated. It becomes like a new creation. Old things are passed away, and all things become new. And though it may retain somewhat of its ancient and original characteristics, nevertheless it is a different kind of sap that is now flowing through its veins,—a different kind of blossom that is bursting forth from its foliage,—a different kind of fruit that is gathered from its branches. In fact, there is a species of conversion. The noxious is turned into the fruitful, and that which, by itself, or in its own nature, was useless, or worse than useless, which was positively pernicious, by being incorporated with a precious or a fruit-bearing tree, is transformed into its likeness, and imbibes its virtuous qualities, and is productive of its very fruit.

So it is with the regeneration of the sinner. By himself, or so long as he remains in his natural condition, he is like a wild olive tree. He brings forth iniquity, and nothing else; for such is his nature; and that nature can never be altered by anything which he can do for himself. He may lop off some of the straggling branches, or devote himself to the accomplishment of something like an external reformation. But that will never change the nature of the tree, or make any alteration in the quality of the fruit. But when he is engrafted into Christ, he acquires a new nature, and so becomes fruitful in good works,—fruitful, not because of any virtue that is inherent in himself, but because of the virtue which appertains to Christ, in whom it hath pleased the Father that all fulness should dwell, and which, being drawn forth and imbibed through the exercise of a true faith, transforms him into the likeness of the Divine image, and converts him into a tree of righteousness, the planting of the Lord, that he might be glorified.

But how is it that the wild olive and the fruit bearing are brought into contact? This is done by the hand of the husbandman, and the material which he employs is a lump of dead clay. The clay is very important; it is absolutely indispensable: but in the clay itself there is no life, no warmth, no vitality. It does not even convey the virtue from the precious to the vile,—from the good olive tree to the wild and sterile. It only binds them close together, and prevents them from being severed by the rains and the tempests of heaven. So it is with faith. Its province is to unite the soul unto Christ, and when that end is accomplished, its office is fulfilled. Yet men are apt to think of it as something altogether different from this,—as something in itself so vital, that, instead of shutting them up into Christ, they allow it to interpose between them, and thereby they frustrate the very object it is intended to serve.

Faith itself they put in the place which ought to be occupied by Christ; and instead of cleaving to the living Saviour, they clasp the dead clay, and their souls remain without life; they experience no comfort; they produce no fruit. The object for which the clay is used in the process of engrafting, is not to interpose between the wild olive and the fruitful. It is to bind them together. When it does that, it accomplishes the end for which it is employed; and the vital essence, meeting with no obstruction from the dead clay, flows freely from the precious into the vile. So it is with faith. Faith does not constitute the very thing on which we are warranted to rest as the ground of our acceptance, or to which we are at liberty to look as the source of our vitality. That is a grievous mistake, into which many fall, and which interposes the mightiest obstacles in the way of their salvation, and which it is exceedingly difficult for any of us to avoid. We are far more apt to occupy ourselves with the operations of our own faith, than with the living and all-sufficient Saviour, towards whom our faith is invited to look; the consequence of which is, that we seek to find a Saviour to ourselves, not in Christ bearing the burden of our iniquities in his own body on the tree, but a Saviour, mainly if not exclusively, in the exercises of our own faith; and thus, though we ourselves may not be aware of it, we are really going about for the establishment of a righteousness of our own.

There is no virtue, no power, no vitality, no saving efficacy in faith itself. The efficacy, and the power, and the virtue are in Christ.

It was faith, for example, that led the wounded Israelite to lift his dying eye to the brazen serpent that Moses erected in the wilderness, and that under the conviction that by simply looking to the uplifted ensign, his mortal malady would be healed. It was faith that prompted the wretched and abandoned prodigal to arise and return to his father, being assured that in his father's house there was enough and to spare for the satisfying of all his wants, and that in his father's heart there was enough and to spare for the forgiveness of all his sins. It was faith that induced the woman with the issue of blood to mingle with the dense multitude that were following upon the footsteps of the Divine Redeemer, and without the speaking of a single word, or the presenting of an audible petition, to stretch forth her emaciated hand, and to touch the hem of his garment. And it was faith that taught the dying malefactor on the cross, to address the prayer of his departing spirit to the Man of Sorrows, whose last agonies were embittered by the railings of his infidel associate, and around whose cross the savage and infuriated mob were lifting up their horrid yells of blasphemy; and that faith comprehended these two things:—first, the deep and thorough conviction that he was a miserable sinner, suffering the just punishment of his crimes and verging on the very brink of eternal perdition;—and second, the deep and thorough conviction, that Christ, even though brought down to the lowest point in the scale of humiliation, with the rough nails in his hands and in his feet, and the lacerations of the crown of thorns on his brow, was nevertheless invested with the prerogatives of a King, —a King who was not only able to save him from going down to the pit, but who could set him at his own right hand, when he was come to his kingdom and was sitting upon his throne. But neither in the case of the wounded Israelite, nor in the case of the abandoned prodigal, nor in the case of the woman with the issue of blood, nor in the case of the dying malefactor on the cross, was there ought of merit or vitality in the faith which they put forth, saving and excepting that only which flowed from the living Saviour on whom it was fixed. Faith unquestionably there was, bringing the soul in its emptiness and misery into close contact with Christ, and shutting it up into him in whom all fulness dwells. But the faith itself was not possessed of any inherent power, nor was it wrought up and elaborated in the soul by means of the tears and the penances of a dark protracted night of sorrow. It was the act of a moment, springing from the conviction, that in themselves they were lost, but that Christ was able and ready to save them;—the act of a moment, which found expression in the glance of a sinner's closing eye, or in the touch of a sinner's trembling hand, or in the brief petition of a sinner's last expiring breath.

Observe, next, where it is that the olive tree flourishes and brings forth fruit abundantly. You might think that this would be the case, in an eminent degree, when it was defended from the violence of every blast, and planted in the richest soil. Yet this does not seem to be indispensable to the growth or the fruitfulness of such a tree. On the contrary, it is often found, spreading forth its branches towards heaven, and laden with the richest fruit, in places where least of all it might have been expected, striking its roots into the clefts of the everlasting rocks, and pouring down fatness on the very ground that is covered with the stones of emptiness, and marked with the bleakness of desolation. Other trees may thrive well, and may bring forth fruit abundantly, when planted in a deep soil, and sheltered from the stormy blast. But the fatness of the olive seems to be more dependent upon the genial influences of heaven, coming down from above, and finding access to its vital parts, through its green leaves and its expanding blossoms, than upon the nourishment which it receives through the instrumentality of its spreading roots, or the rich juices which it gathers underneath the ground. It is a tree which rejoices in the bright sunshine, as if it drew its sustenance from the elements of hea ven, and therefore, though all around and beneath it may present the aspect of a dry and thirsty land, where there is neither fertility of soil, nor fountains abounding with living water, nevertheless, even there it is fat, and full of sap, and flourishing.

Is it the case that the olive tree thus thrives amid the waste places of the wilderness, deriving the main elements of its vitality from above, and imbibing oil apparently even out of the flinty rock? So is it with the saint whose soul is truly united unto Christ, and whose conversation or whose citizenship is in heaven. His vitality is not dependent, mainly or exclusively, on the soil that is beneath his feet,—on the nourishment which he derives from earth, or from earthly things, —on the materials which he gathers amid the occupations and the enjoyments of this lower world. His spirit within him is nourished and sustained by the hidden manna,—by the heavenly influences that come down to him in silence and without observation from the sanctuary that is above,—by the spiritual bread, of which if a man eat he shall never hunger,—by the living water, of which if a man drink he shall never thirst, but which shall be in him as a well of water, springing up into everlasting life. And hence, his fruitfulness is not most apparent when all things outwardly are going well with him, and he seems to be walking under the sunshine of great worldly prosperity. At such seasons the graces of the Spirit are rather apt to languish and decay, and leanness and meagreness to enter into his soul. It is when the bleakness of the wilderness is around him, and the roots under ground are obstructed by the hard and flinty rock, that he spreads forth his branches overhead, and regales himself with the dews and the genial influences that come down upon him from above. In fact, he is in a measure independent of the temporal and adventitious advantages to which worldly men are looking for the main elements of their felicity. He has food to eat which the world knows not of, and joys with which a stranger cannot intermeddle; and these, for the most part, the richest and the most abundant when all other joys are gone,—light shining out of the dark cloud,—sweetness mingled with the bitter cup,—the oil of gladness oozing out of the flinty rock,—the door of hope set open in the valley of Achor,—the vision of guardian angels amid the gloom of the sepulchre,—the lights of a glorious immortality swallowing up the dark shadows of death. "Although the fig-tree shall not blossom, neither shall fruit be in the vines; the labour of the olive shall fail, and the fields shall yield no meat; the flock shall be cut off from the fold, and there shall be no herd in the stalls: yet I will rejoice in the Lord, I will joy in the God of my salvation."*

* Habakkuk iii. 17, 18.

Observe still farther the purposes to which the fruit of the olive tree was applied. A rich oil was extracted out of it, which, besides being used for common purposes, was likewise employed for the consecration of the priests under the law, and for imparting a sweet smelling odour to the oblations which were presented on the altar, and also, and more especially, for feeding the lamps of the golden candlestick, and thereby lighting up the dark tabernacle with the lustre of a brilliant illumination.

Now this applies, first of all, to Christ himself, the consecrated one, who was anointed with the oil of gladness above his fellows, and whose name is like ointment poured forth. He is the great High Priest who holds the stars in his right hand, and who walks amid the lustre of the golden candlestick. And hence the meaning of the vision which was seen by the prophet Zechariah:—"And the angel that talked with me came again, and waked me, as a man that is wakened out of his sleep, and said unto me, What seest thou? And I said, I have looked, and behold a candlestick all of gold, with a bowl upon the top of it, and his seven lamps thereon, and seven pipes to the seven lamps, which are upon the top thereof: and two olive trees by it, one upon the right side of the bowl, and the other upon the left side thereof . . . Then answered I, and said unto him, What are these two olive trees upon the right side of the candlestick, and upon the left side thereof? . . . And what be these two olive branches which through the two golden pipes empty the golden oil out of themselves? . . . Then said he, These are the two anointed ones, that stand by the Lord of the whole earth."*

Now, without stopping to inquire into the primary application of this vision, if we suppose that the two anointed ones, which the olive trees represent, are descriptive of Christ, and of the Holy Spirit that proceeds from him, then it suggests this interesting and important idea, that all the light that shines through the sanctuary, and all the fragrant incense that is mingled with the services of the saints, and all the rich and everlasting consolations which are to be found in the ordinances of God's appointment, are not necessarily connected with the services themselves, but flow forth, in heavenly influences, or through channels of gold, from the fulness of a living Saviour, and from the plentiful effusions of his blessed Spirit. Let the olive trees be cut down, let the golden pipes be broken, let the supplies of the sacred oil be stopped; and straightway the lamps of the tabernacle would be extinguished, and Ichabod might be inscribed on the gates of every sanctuary, and on the horns of every altar; for henceforth the light and the glory are away. It is the presence of the anointed ones that gives to the Bible all its vitality,

* Zech. iv. 1—14.

and to the promises all their sweetness, and to the Gospel all its efficacy, and to the ordinances of the sanctuary all their preciousness and all their power. And hence the language of Christ himself:—"The Spirit of the Lord God is upon me; because the Lord hath anointed me to preach good tidings unto the meek; he hath sent me to bind up the broken-hearted, to proclaim liberty to the captives, and the opening of the prison to them that are bound; to proclaim the acceptable year of the Lord, and the day of vengeance of our God; to comfort all that mourn; to appoint unto them that mourn in Zion, to give unto them beauty for ashes, the oil of joy for mourning, the garment of praise for the spirit of heaviness; that they might be called trees of righteousness, the planting of the Lord, that he might be glorified."*

But if Christ is the source and the channel of all heavenly influences—if it is from him, and the Spirit that proceeds from him, that there cometh down every good and every perfect gift, it comes next to be an interesting inquiry, What was the process which Christ himself had to undergo, before it was competent for these vital influences to flow forth to us?

This brings us back again to the olive tree, which furnishes the materials for a striking and memorable illustration. The illustration

* Isaiah lxi. 1—3.

is this: When the olive berries were fully ripe, it was the practice in ancient times to shake them off from the tree, or to beat them down with rods. They were then gathered together, and trodden under foot as in a winepress, or bruised and sore broken by the action of machinery, the result of which was that the oil, being extracted out of the berry, was treasured up in earthen vessels which were sunk into the earth, and which remained there till the sediment fell to the bottom, and the oil, purified and refined, was in a fit condition to be used.

Need we observe how faithfully this process has been exemplified in the case of Christ? He himself exclaims, "I am feeble and sore broken." "Thy hand presseth me sore." "I am poured out like water, and all my bones are out of joint." "My strength is dried up like a potsherd." "My tongue cleaveth to my jaws." "I am like a broken vessel." "And thou hast brought me unto the dust of death."* And because he was thus wounded for our transgressions, and bruised for our iniquities, the oil of joy is not only provided in rich and plentiful abundance, but is actually poured forth into earthen vessels, and vessels of wrath that were fit only for perdition, turning them, first of all, into vessels of mercy, and hereafter into vessels of everlasting glory.

But whilst this was the case in an eminent

* Psalms xxii., xxxi., xxxviii.

degree with Christ himself, it is so also, though in a subordinate sense, with the members of his body. God does not leave them altogether unto themselves, even when they are bringing forth fruit. The olive berries must be crushed and broken to pieces, not with the view of destroying them, but for the purpose of separating the pure oil from the grosser elements with which it is mingled, and thereby making it ready for the Master's use. It may seem to be a stern process. But it is needful; and, as it is with many other things, a blessing comes out of it. It is the broken rock that sends forth streams of living water through the wilderness. It is the broken ground that opens its bosom for the reception of the incorruptible seed which springs up and which brings forth fruit abundantly. It is the broken cloud that discharges itself in showers that usher in the spring, and cheer the thirsty ground. It is the broken alabaster wherewith the poor penitent anoints the feet of the Saviour, and which fills the whole house with the odour of the precious spikenard. It is the broken body which the nails of the cross and the spear of a mortal enemy have pierced, that furnishes the blood that cleanses the soul from all sin. It is the broken veil that opens into the holiest of all, and gives to the believing soul bright glimpses into the glory that is yet to be revealed. It is the broken grave that announces the reality of the resurrection, and proclaims to the unbelieving disciple that the Saviour is risen indeed. It is the broken corn that is separated from the chaff, and laid up in the garner of the husbandman, or changed into the bread of life. And it is the broken berries which the millstones of the olive press have crushed, that give forth the precious oil which fills the dark tabernacle with the radiance of a clear and tranquillizing light.

So it is with vital Christians. It is by means of the sifting and the crushing processes to which they are subjected by the providence of God, that they become like the salt of the earth—like the lamps of the tabernacle—like the lights of the world. The holy oil, the sacred influences they derive from Christ. These are not inherent in themselves. They come down "from the Father of lights, with whom is no variableness neither shadow of turning." Nevertheless they are the instruments, as in the case of a candlestick, by which the light is diffused, by which it is scattered abroad; and when they are found holding forth the word of righteousness in the midst of a crooked and perverse generation, amongst whom they are called to shine as lights in the world, they are the means of doing much good, even during the course of this brief and mortal life, or while occupied with the ordinances of the Tabernacle upon earth.

Thus much for the oil with which the fruit of the Olive tree abounds. Even though used for a temporary purpose, it was of great value; for it fed the lamps of the golden candlestick, and thereby served to bring into visible manifestation both the officiating priest and the provisions of the table of shew-bread, with the sacred utensils, and the rich furniture, with which the Tabernacle was adorned.

But the Tabernacle was not meant to be permanent. It was a temporary erection, adapted to the circumstances of God's people, while they were passing through the wilderness. There was another edifice which was at once figurative of better things to come, and destined to be more enduring; we mean the Temple which was built at Jerusalem, or within the precincts of the promised land.

Now it is deserving of notice that the fruit which the Olive tree produces was not only used in the service of the Tabernacle, which could be done while the tree itself was yet growing; but after the tree was cut down, when the vitality was gone out of it, when it was incapable of bringing forth fruit any more, still even in that state it was not thrown aside, as if it were altogether useless, but being subjected to the tools of the cunning artificer, and carved into figures of exquisite beauty, it formed a part, and a most important part, in the splendid and magnificent Temple, where the name of God was recorded, and unto which the tribes of Israel went up; insomuch that it was impossible for any one to enter into the Temple at all, or into the most holy place, without passing between the side-posts, or the pillars, that were cut out of the Olive tree, and carved into the figures of the cherubim, that were overlaid with gold.

And wherefore was it that this kind of wood was employed for this special purpose? The reason probably was this. The Olive tree, from time immemorial, has been recognized as the ensign of peace, or of reconciliation, or of good-will; and this it is by no means unlikely may have arisen from the fact, that it was a leaf of the Olive tree plucked off which the dove brought as the messenger of good tidings to the ark, and which seemed to intimate to the prisoners of hope that were within, that the wrath of Almighty God was appeased, and that the waters were abated from off the face of the whole earth. And when the materials of the same tree were made use of, both at the outer door of the Temple and at the entrance to the holy oracle, it seemed to intimate that a way of access has not only been opened into the holiest of all, but that this is emphatically a way of peace, or of reconciliation. For this is the language of an apostle, applicable to the case of all true believers, Gentiles as well as Jews:—"Now, in Christ Jesus, ye who sometimes were far off, are made nigh by the blood of Christ. For he is our peace, who hath made both one, and hath broken down the middle wall of partition between us; having abolished in his flesh the enmity, even the law of commandments contained in ordinances; for to make in himself of twain one new man, so making peace; and that he might reconcile both unto God in one body by the cross, having slain the enmity thereby; and came and preached peace to you which were afar off, and to them that were nigh. For through him we both have access by one Spirit unto the Father. Now therefore ye are no more strangers and foreigners, but fellow-citizens with the saints, and of the household of God; and are built upon the foundation of the apostles and prophets, Jesus Christ himself being the chief corner-stone; in whom all the building fitly framed together groweth unto an holy temple in the Lord: in whom ye also are builded together for an habitation of God through the Spirit." *

Therefore, if you are vital Christians, bringing forth ripened fruit, you will not only be the instruments of shedding floods of light through the tabernacle on earth, which is meant to be temporary, but even after you are dead, you will enter into the holiest of all through the rent veil of the Redeemer's flesh, and may yourselves be formed into side-posts or pillars in the heavenly temple, which is illuminated with the glory of God and the Lamb—pillars that shall go no more out, that shall never be removed like the stakes of the temporary Tabernacle, but which shall stand forever as monuments of the Divine mercy, inscribed with the name of the living God, and overshadowed with

* Eph. ii. 13—22.

the cherubim who rest not day and night, crying unto one another, "Holy, holy, holy is the Lord of Hosts; the heavens and the earth are full of his glory."

It is a great matter to be lights shining in the tabernacle that is on earth: it is a greater matter to be pillars in the temple of God that is in heaven. The one as well as the other we may be through Christ, the good Olive tree, into whom all true believers are engrafted by faith, and on whom they are dependent for the enjoyment of all their present privileges, and for the prospect and the realization of the coming glory.

Are you then united unto Christ, or are you standing isolated and apart by yourselves? If apart by yourselves you can neither be productive of good fruit in the present life, nor will you be found hereafter, either as pillars embellishing the celestial temple, or as brilliant jewels in the Saviour's blood bought crown. Separated from Christ you are without life, without hope, without fruit—useless, or worse than useless—positively pernicious, fit only to be cut down as cumberers of the ground, and cast into the fire and burned.

But if you are engrafted into Christ you cannot be destroyed. You can never perish. You may be trodden as in a wine-press, or crushed by the pressure of many heavy trials. The axe, the hammer, the chisel, the plane, the fire, may be all brought to bear upon you. But these will be the instruments of doing you no real harm. They will only rid you of your imperfections, and mould you into the likeness of the Divine image, and bring you into conformity with the heavenly pattern, and prepare you for being pillars amid the glories of that celestial temple, which is paved with transparent gold, and garnished from the walls to the very foundations with all manner of most precious stones, and where they need no candle, neither light of the sun nor of the moon to shine in it: for the glory of God doth lighten it, and the Lamb is the light thereof.

THE

CHURCH IN THE HOUSE.

BY THE

Rev. JAMES HAMILTON,

MINISTER OF THE FREE CHURCH, REGENT SQUARE, LONDON

"Wherever I have a Tent, there God shall have an Altar."—*John Howard.*

PHILADELPHIA:
PRESBYTERIAN BOARD OF PUBLICATION.

Greet the Church that is in their house.—Rom. xvi. 5.

Again I say unto you that if two of you shall agree on earth as touching any thing that they shall ask, it shall be done for them of my Father which is in heaven. For where two or three are gathered together in my name, there am I in the midst of them.—Matt. xviii. 19, 20.

Let the word of Christ dwell in you richly in all wisdom: teaching and admonishing one another in psalms, and hymns, and spiritual songs, singing with grace in your hearts, to the Lord.—Col. iii. 16.

I know him (Abraham) that he will command his children and his household after him, and they shall keep the way of the Lord.—Gen. xviii. 19.

The voice of rejoicing and salvation is in the tabernacles of the righteous.—Psalm cxviii. 15.

THE CHURCH IN THE HOUSE.

IN Greenland, when a stranger knocks at the door, he asks, " Is God in this house ?" And if they answer, " Yes ;" he enters. Reader, this little messenger knocks at your door with the Greenland salutation. Is GOD IN THIS HOUSE ? Were you like Abraham, entertaining an angel unawares, what would be the report he would take back to heaven ? Would he find you commanding your children and your household, and teaching them the way of the Lord? Would he find an altar in your dwelling ? Do you worship God with your children ? Is there *a Church in your house ?*

If not, then God is not in your house. A prayerless family is a godless family. It is worse. It is a family on which Jehovah frowns. He will pour out his fury upon it some day. " O Lord, pour out thy fury upon the heathen that know thee not, and upon the families that call not on thy name."* A prayerless family and a heathen family are here accounted the same.

I cannot mention all the reasons in favour

* Jer. x. 25.

of family worship; but if you ponder them, the four following should suffice:—

1. The godly householders mentioned in Scripture practised it. Would you desire to be like Abraham the friend of God? Wherever he pitched his tent, he builded an altar, and called on the name of the Lord;* and Jehovah declared, concerning him, "I know Abraham, that he will command his children and his household after him, and they will keep the way of the Lord."† Would you like to resemble Job, "the perfect and upright man, one that feared God and eschewed evil?" He used to bring his children together, and rose early in the morning, and offered a sacrifice of as many victims as he had sons and daughters, teaching us how express and special our intercession for our families should be, and this he did "continually."‡ Would you resemble David, the man after God's own heart? At the close of a busy day, we find him going "home to bless his household."§ Do you envy Cornelius, whose prayers were heard, and to whom the Lord sent a special messenger to teach him the way of salvation? He was "a devout man, one who feared God *with all his house*, and prayed to God always;" and who was so anxious for the salvation of his family, that he got together his kinsmen and near friends

* Gen. xii. 7, 8 xiii. 4, 8.
† Gen. xviii. 19
‡ Job i. 5, 8.
§ 1 Chron. xvi. 43.

that they might be ready to hear the apostle when he arrived, and share with himself the benefit.* Do you admire Aquila and Priscilla, Paul's "helpers in Christ Jesus," and who were so skilful in the Scriptures, that they were able to teach a young minister the way of God more perfectly? You will find that one reason for their familiarity with Scripture was, that they had "a Church in their house."† In the Bible you find instances of family devotion in all ranks of life, from the king to the artisan, from David's palace to the tent of Aquila; to teach you that whatever be your situation in life, you should still have a Church in your house. I have sometimes seen family worship in great houses; but I have felt that God was quite as near when I knelt with a praying family on the earthen floor of their cottage. I have known of family worship among the reapers in a barn. It used to be common in the fishing-boats upon the friths and lakes of Scotland. I have heard of its being observed in the depths of a coal-pit. I scarcely know the situation in life in which a willing family might not contrive to pray together. If you live in a scoffing ungodly neighbourhood, so much the better. Abraham built his altar whilst heathen Canaanites looked on. He lifted up a testimony for God, and God honoured him so that Abimelech, his neighbour was con-

* Acts x. 2, 24, 31, 33.
† Acts xviii. 26; Rom. xvi. 5.

strained to say, "God is with thee in all that thou doest."*

2. Wherever religion revives, family worship abounds. When the Spirit is poured out upon the house of David, "the land shall mourn, every *family* apart."† I can remember no instance of a great revival, of which this was not an attendant sign. Listen to the account which Mr. Baxter gives of Kidderminster during his ministry. "On the Lord's day there was no disorder to be seen in the streets, but you might hear a hundred families singing psalms and repeating sermons, as you passed through the streets. When I came thither first, there was about one family in a street that worshipped God and called on his name, and when I came away, there were some streets, where there was not above one family in the side of a street that did not so; and that did not by professing serious godliness give us some hopes of their sincerity: and those families which were the worst, being inns and alehouses, usually some persons in each did seem to be religious. Some of the poor men did competently understand the body of divinity, and were able to judge in difficult controversies. Some of them were so able in prayer that very few ministers did match them in order, and fulness and apt expressions, and holy oratory with fervency. Abundance of them were able to pray very laud

* Gen. xxi. 22. † Zech. x. 12.

ably with their families, or with others. The temper of their minds and the innocency of their lives was much more laudable than their parts." When the Spirit is poured upon us, our cities will all present a similar aspect.

3. It would make your home much happier if you had a church in your house. It has been said with much truth, "Family prayer is the oil which removes friction and causes all the complicated wheels of the family to move smoothly and noiselessly." It is one way, and the very best, for bringing all the members of a family together, and for promoting that harmony of feeling so essential to domestic enjoyment. Some families are held together by hardly any bond, except that they lodge under the same roof, and assemble round the same board. But when they meet, it is not to fulfil one another's joy. They are selfish and sullen; cross words, peevish answers, and angry recriminations make up all their intercourse. The customary meal is despatched in a gloomy silence, or embittered by fretful words. I have known families so little a home with one another, that it was quite a relief when any casual visiter dropped in to break the irksomeness of their own society. I have seen brothers and sisters so ill-assorted in the families in which God had planted them together, that they had no subject of common interest and no mutual love nor confidence. They could converse and be happy

with strangers, but not with one another And I have seen this in families where there was a form of family worship,—a pretence, a semblance of prayer—but never where there was the reality. If yours be such a family, before peace and affection visit it, you must say, "Come and let us seek the Lord." If you would see the dawn of blander days on that clouded and lowering circle, you must cry, "Lord, lift thou up the light of thy countenance upon us, and so we shall be glad." If you could only persuade them to take into their hands the volume that speaks good will to man, and as they sit together to read by turns its messages of kindness; and then as they bowed before the mercy-seat, if in their common name, you said, *Our Father*, and confessed their common sins, returned thanks for any mercies which the day had brought, and asked such blessings as all need, this process could not be long persisted in, till you would see its softening and harmonizing influence. The dew of Hermon would begin to come down, and you would exclaim as you saw the difference, "Behold how good and how pleasant it is for brethren to dwell together in unity."*

But perhaps your family dwells in unity—but it is not a holy unity. It is not sanctified by the word of God and by prayer. You are happy in one another. You are never at a loss for the materials of a cheerful inter-

* Psalm cxxxiii

course. But amidst all the sprightliness, and cordiality, and kind feeling which encompass your fireside, one ingredient of gladness is wanting. God is forgotten. In the morning you meet and give one another a joyous greeting, and, the morning meal despatched, rush away to the day's engagements without a word of acknowledgment to that God whose sleepless eye guarded your midnight pillow —without one word of prayer to bespeak his upholding and guidance in this day's untrodden path. And when the evening hour of intercourse is over, and you have discussed the pleasant or prosperous incidents of the day, you hie away, *cheerful* but *unthankful*, to a prayerless slumber, perhaps to awake in death's dark valley, and find that the Lord is not with you. Your family is united—but it is a short-lived union. Your family-love—God is not in it, and therefore heaven does not follow after it. How it would give tone and intensity to the affection of your smiling circle, if you could be brought to love one another *in the Lord!* With what new eyes you would learn to look upon yourselves, if you came to regard one another as brethren for eternity! And how it would heighten bliss, and take the sharpness out of sorrow, if "for ever with the Lord," were the thought which joy and grief most readily suggested! Were it manifest of all the members of a family that God is their Father, Christ their elder Brother, and the Holy Spirit their Comforter, such a family would possess a joy which the removal of no member could take away. That joy has often come into households through the channel of domestic devotion. For,

4. Family worship is an ordinance which God has often blessed to the saving of souls. In houses where it is conducted with life and feeling, it has often proved a converting ordinance. A few years ago, an English gentleman visited America, and spent some days with a pious friend. He was a man of talent and accomplishments, but an infidel. Four years afterwards he returned to the same house, a Christian. They wondered at the change, but little suspected when and where it had originated. He told them that when he was present at their family worship, on the first evening of his former visit, and when after the chapter was read, they all knelt down to pray—the recollection of such scenes in his father's house long years ago, rushed in on his memory, so that he did not hear a single word. But the occurrence made him *think*, and his thoughtfulness ended in his leaving the howling wilderness of infidelity, and finding a quiet rest in the salvation wrought out by Jesus Christ. In his *Fireside*, Mr. Abbot tells us of a gay young lady who paid a visit of a week in the family of a minister, an eminently holy man. His fervent intercessions for his children and the other inmates of his dwelling, went to this thoughtless heart: they were the Spirit's arrow, and upon that family

altar, his visiter was enabled to present herself a living sacrifice to God. It is with the Church in the house as with the church in the village. The wayfarer may get a word in passing, which he never can forget. The stranger that turns aside to tarry for a night may hear at your family worship a word that will save his soul. Some years ago, an Irish wanderer, his wife, and his sister, asked a night's shelter in the cabin of a pious schoolmaster. With the characteristic hospitality of his nation, the schoolmaster made them welcome. It was his hour for evening worship, and when the strangers were seated, he began by reading slowly and solemnly, the second chapter of the Epistle to the Ephesians. The young man sat astonished. The expressions, "dead in trespasses and sins," "children of wrath," "walking after the course of this world," were new to him. He sought an explanation. He was told that this is God's account of the state of man by nature. He felt that it was exactly his own state. "In this way I have walked from my childhood. In the service of the god of this world we have come to your house." He was on the way to a fair, where he intended to pass a quantity of counterfeit money. But God's word had found him out. He produced his store of coin, and begged his host to cast in into the fire; and asked anxiously if he could not obtain the word of God for himself. His request was complied with, and next morning, with the new treasure, the party, who had now no errand to the fair, returned to their own home. Perhaps, by this time, the pious schoolmaster has met his guest within the gates of the city, outside of which are thieves, and whatsoever maketh a lie. But I cannot enumerate all the conversions which have occurred at the Church in the house. Many servants have been awakened there. Children have often heard there truths, which, when the Spirit brought them to remembrance, in after days—perhaps, in days of profligacy, and when far from their father's house—have sent home the prodigal. It is not only of Zion's solemn assemblies, but of Jacob's humble dwellings—the little fireside sanctuaries—that the Lord shall count, when he writeth up the people, "This man was born there." In your house there have been, perhaps, several immortal spirits born into the world. Have there been any born again?

Prayerless parents! Your irreligion may prove your children's damnation. They might have been within the fold of the Saviour by this time, had not you hindered them when entering in. That time when God visited your family with a heavy stroke, they were thoughtful for a season, but there was no Church in your house to give a heavenly direction to that thoughtfulness, and it soon died away. That evening when they came home from the Sabbath School so serious, if you had been a pious father or mother, you would have taken your boy aside, and spoken tenderly to him, and asked what his teacher had been telling him, and you would have prayed with him, and tried to deepen the impression. But your children came in from the Church or school, and found no Church in their father's house. Their hearts were softened, but your worldliness soon hardened them. The seed of the kingdom was just springing in their souls and by this time might have been a rich harvest of salvation; but in the atmosphere of your ungodly house, the tender blade withered instantly. Your idle talk, your frivolity your Sunday visiters, your prayerless evening, ruined all. Your children were coming to Christ, and you suffered them not. And you will not need to hinder them long. The carnal mind is enmity against God; but no enmity so deep as theirs who were almost reconciled and then drew back. You drove your children back. You hardened them. They may never more be moved. They may grow up as prayerless and ungodly as yourself. If God should change you, they may soon be too hard for your own tears and entreaties. If you die as you are, their evil works will follow you to the world of woe, and pour new ingredients into your own cup of wrath. Oh! think of these things. A prayerless house is not only a cheerless one, but it is a guilty one; for where God is not, there Satan is.

But I know not why I should multiply words to prove a duty which nature teaches,

The poor Pagan, with his household gods and family altar, will rise in the judgment against some of this generation and will condemn them. Instead, therefore, of saying more on the obligation and advantages of this most reasonable service, I shall endeavour to give some plain directions to those into whose hearts the Lord has put the desire to begin it.

1. Can you sing? or is there any one in the house who can? You will find it enliven the service wonderfully if you can make "a joyful noise unto the Lord." The psalm or hymn is a part of the service which the youngest enjoy, and in which they will gladly take a share.

2. There is the reading of the word of God. You may go straight through, or you may select a course of subjects. For instance, you might read the parables as one series, and the miracles of Christ as another. You might select the biographical portions, and read the lives of Adam, Noah, Abraham, Peter, Paul, &c; or you might read the Epistles in connection with the history of the Churches or individuals to whom they are addressed. Thus you might compare Ephesians with Acts xviii.—xx., and with Rev. ii. 1—8; or Thessalonians with Acts xvii. 1—13; and you might compare the Psalms with the period in David's history when each was written, and the Prophecies with those passages which record their fulfilment—a comparison, which a Bible, with good marginal

references, will enable you to make. Or you may select passages appropriate to particular seasons. On the morning of a Lord's day, you might read Psalm xlviii., lxiii., lxxxiv., xcii., cxviii.; John xx.; Rev. i., &c. On a sacramental Sabbath, Psalm xxii., xlv.; Isa. liii.; Matt. xxvi.; John vi., &c. It might help to keep attention awake, if each read a verse in rotation. At other times there might be more solemnity if the same person read the whole continuously. It would make it more impressive and more memorable, if you occasionally asked a question, or made a few remarks on the passage read. For instance, you read the nineteenth of Luke, and this is your commentary as you go along.

1. "And Jesus entered and passed through Jericho.
2. "And behold there was a man named Zaccheus, which was the chief among the publicans (or tax-gatherers,) and he was rich.
3. "And he sought to see Jesus, who he was: and could not for the press, because he was little of stature."

This was the last time that Jesus passed through Jericho. He had often passed quietly through it before; but now his time was fully come, and he could not be hid. The road was full of passengers at this season at any rate; for it was Passover time, and they were all going up to Jerusalem. Besides, the sensation in Jericho was increased by the miracle which Jesus had just wrought on the blind beggar, and which we read in the last chapter yesterday. The crowd was so great that Zaccheus could get no opening to push through, and he was so little that he could not see over other people's shoulders.

4. "And he ran before, and climbed up into a sycamore tree to see him: for he was to pass that way.
5. "And when Jesus came to the place he looked up, and saw him, and said unto him, Zaccheus, make haste, and come down; for to-day I must abide at thy house."

How surprised he must have been! Up in the leafy sycamore, he never expected to be noticed. But see! Jesus stands still and looks at him as if he were about to speak. Perhaps Zaccheus expected to get a rebuke before the multitude for his villanies, when Jesus, in his own gentle way, just says, "Zaccheus, make haste, and come down; for to-day I must abide at thy house." Grace went with the word.

6. "And he made haste, and came down, and received him joyfully.
7. "And when they saw it, they all murmured, saying, That he was gone to be guest with a man that is a sinner."

There were many who felt that they had a better right to this distinction than the mean, grasping tax-gatherer. Many of them felt as if they were not SINNERS. It lowered their opinion of Christ, that he would condescend to become the guest of such a man. They little knew the reason.

8. "And Zaccheus stood, and said unto the Lord, Behold, Lord, the half of my goods I give to the poor:

and if I have taken any thing from any man by false accusation, I restore him fourfold."

How glad he must have been! A happy heart devises liberal things—and so happy had this visit made him, that his greedy soul had no longer love for money. He stood up like one on whom a sudden thought had come, or who wished to give solemnity to what he said, and declared that he would make it all up to those whom he had wronged, and give half his substance to the poor. This was the effect of receiving Jesus. Where the love of Christ enters, the love of the world goes out. What would the murmurers think when they saw this change upon the "sinner?"

9. "And Jesus said unto him, This day is salvation come to this house, forasmuch as he also is a son of Abraham."

It was his "joyful receiving" of Jesus which made him a son of Abraham. It made him more. It made him one of the sons of God.* Have we received Christ? Has his voice ever made us joyful? Have we ever parted with "goods," or any thing else from gratitude to Him? Now let us remember the next verse, for it is one of Christ's own faithful sayings.

10. "For the Son of Man is come to seek and to save that which was lost."

This is one way. Another, and perhaps

* John i. 12.

better way, is to make the members of the family supply the commentary themselves. This evening, before it is so late that you are all sleepy, you sit round the table, each with his Bible open before him; and the passage selected is the forty-fifth of Isaiah.

1. "Thus saith the Lord to his anointed, to Cyrus, whose right hand I have holden, to subdue nations before him; and I will loose the loins of kings to open before him the two-leaved gates; and the gates shall not be shut."

Father. The prophet has been foretelling the fall of Babylon, and here he names its conqueror. Mary, what is his name?

Mary. Cyrus.

Father. Does any one know how long after this it was before Cyrus made his appearance?—Can no one tell? George, your Bible has got the date on its margin. Can you tell when Isaiah uttered this prophecy?

George. About 712 years before Christ.

Father. Now if you will look to the beginning of Ezra, you will see the first year of Cyrus set down there.

George. Before Christ 536.

Father. Then how long before had the Lord called Cyrus by his name?

George. Nearly 200 years.

Father. It is not very long since John and Henry finished the "Life of Cyrus." Do you remember any facts which illustrate this prophecy?

Henry. The Lord says, "I have holden his right hand to subdue nations before him."

Cyrus subdued the Lydians with their rich King Crœsus, the Phrygians, the Phœnicians, and many more, as well as the Babylonians.

John. Yes; and when he took Babylon, "the gates were not shut." For the people were all drinking and diverting themselves, when he dried up the river; and had forgot to shut the gates at the end of the streets which open into the river—so that Cyrus had nothing to do but march down the dry channel, and then climb up the banks into the city.

Father. Very true—but do you remember nothing more about "opening the two-leaved gates?"

Henry. Oh, yes! When the king of Babylon heard the uproar in the city, he sent to find out what was the matter, and when they were opening the palace gates to let out the king's messenger, the Persians rushed in and killed the king.

Try to bring out some lesson that may be needed that very day. You read at morning worship that verse, 1 Cor. x. 31.

"Whether, therefore, ye eat or drink, or whatsoever ye do, do all to the glory of God."

Father. What does that mean?

John. That every thing, however little, we are to do so as to please God.

Father. Quite so. It means that you, children, when learning your lessons or at play—that Sarah down stairs, and your father in his counting room, should all remember that we have a Father in Heaven, and should do *every* thing, the little things and the great things, in the way that pleases Him.

Mother. This was the principle on which Oberlin acted. Here is a passage which I marked, when I read his life not long ago.

"The views of religion which Oberlin entertained, made him bring the greatest principles to the minutest operation. He would take a stone out of the road, if it were likely to incommode a traveller, on the principle of love to his neighbour; and in this manner he argued respecting all the duties in which mankind are engaged. Take, for instance, a direction to his people on planting trees. This, with other men, would be an affair of convenience; with him, in his circumstances, it was a religious duty. He thus addressed his parishioners:—

"*November* 18*th*, 1803.

"Dear Friends,

"Satan the enemy of mankind, rejoices when we demolish and destroy. Our Lord Jesus Christ, on the contrary, rejoices when we labour for the public good. You all desire to be saved by him, and hope to become partakers of his glory. Please Him, then, by every possible means, during the remainder of the time you may have to live in this world. He is pleased, when, from the principle of love, you plant trees for the public benefit. Now is the season. Be willing, then, to plant them. Plant them also in the best possible manner. Remember you do it to please him. Put all your roads into good condition; ornament them; employ some of your trees for this purpose, and attend to their growth."

Father. Well, let us do like Oberlin. Let us be kind, and obliging, and useful; and remember that nothing is so little, but that we may do it to the glory of God.

The passage which you mean to read with your family, read carefully over beforehand; and consider what are its most striking points and most useful lessons: and a little practice will make you a good family expositor.

3. The last and most important part of family worship is united prayer. By prayer, I mean the outpouring of an earnest heart in the name of Jesus. It is not prayer when you merely read or repeat a heartless form. You do not ask a blessing on your daily bread, when you merely mutter over it a charm—a few inarticulate words for custom's sake. Nor do you pray when you bend the knee, and read or say a few petitions which you do not feel, and which you forget as soon as you have uttered. It is prayer, when you ask from God blessings which you are really anxious to obtain, and when, in a conviction of your own unworthiness, you ask them for the sake of Him who indeed is worthy, the well beloved Son of God. It is prayer, when you ask so earnestly that you remember afterwards what you sought, and so believingly, that, looking up, you expect an answer. Be earnest. Better no prayer, than give your family a distaste at prayer, by your dulness and formality. Be honest. Deal truly with the God of Truth. Do not mock the Searcher of hearts. Give yourself to the Lord—then set up his worship.

Go to the Lord Jesus yourself, and then seek to bring your children with you.

In family prayer you may be more minute and specific than it is possible to be in more public services. If you have a deep reverence of God upon your mind, there is no fear that particularity will degenerate into an unholy familiarity. If any of your friends are in affliction, pray for them. If your children are at school, or at a Sabbath-class, pray for their teacher. Pray for your brethren in church-fellowship, that the beauty of the Lord may be upon them, and that they may dwell in love. Pray for the office-bearers of your Church; pray for your minister. Endeavour to interest your family in the extension of the Redeemer's kingdom, and pray for faithful ministers and missionaries, especially in those places in which you feel most interested. Every morning commit your way to God. Bespeak his presence in all the duties and temptations of the day—his blessing on your intercourse; and especially on any means of grace, which you hope to enjoy. Every night commend yourselves to his watchful keeping, that you may sleep and wake with him. Pray over the Scriptures you have read. And abound in thanksgiving. Cultivate a cheerful and a grateful spirit: think if there be any mercies you have lately received, and acknowledge them. Has any one arrived from a journey safe and well? Is a sick member of the family restored? Have you heard good news from the far country, tidings from the absent brother? Were you at church or at the prayer meeting this evening, and did you find it refreshing? Have you read in your "Missionary Magazine" the conversion of a heathen or a Jew? Have you heard that God is pouring out his Spirit on some corner of our own country? Have you got an answer to a former prayer? Praise the Lord, for it is pleasant.

It will depend on the age of your family and the amount of your leisure, how long the service should be. Some hurry it over in a way which shows that they have no heart in it themselves. Others prolong it so, that every one else is wearied. Ten minutes of a formal service will look longer than twice the time when the whole soul is in it.

Be consistent. "Behave yourself wisely in a perfect way. Walk within your house with a perfect heart."* If you be devout in prayer, and unholy in practice; if you be heavenly-minded at the hour of worship, and frivolous or proud, or passionate all the day; if you teach your children in the morning, "Be not conformed to this world," and if half the day's lessons be designed to conform them to the world as nearly as possible; if you pray for your household that you may be all meek, and gentle, and kindly-affectioned one to another, and then treat your servants as haughtily as if they were your

* Psalm ci. 2.

slaves or your enemies; your contradictory prayers and practices will be a terrible stumbling-block in their way to the kingdom. God may convert them; but your conduct will make that miracle of grace more surprising still.

Reader, I do not know whether by this time you are almost persuaded or have actually determined to begin. When I think what you are losing who are strangers to this delightful exercise, and when I further think on the blessed results which might flow from your now beginning it, I am loath to leave off—though it is time we were done. Do you still hesitate? What is your excuse?

"I never saw the advantages you describe. It has always been a dull service wherever I have seen it." But *you* need not make it dull. Throw your whole heart and soul into it, and it will be lively enough. It is often dull because it is a mere form. Do you make it a living service, and it will not be dull. It is often dull because it is tedious. Do not spin it out. Better one paragraph of Scripture, feelingly and intelligently read, than a whole chapter listlessly drawled over. Better a prayer no longer than the publican's,* if the whole soul be in it, than a weary form without feeling. Be fervent, and you will not be dull. Family prayer has often been so conducted, that instead of wearying at it, children felt it a punishment to be excluded.

* Luke xviii. 13.

I was once told of a cottage patriarch who was born in those days, when Scotland had a Church in almost every house. There was one in his father's dwelling; and when he pitched a tent for himself he builded an altar. Round that altar a goodly number of olive plants grew up, but, one by one they were either planted out in families of their own, or God took them, till he and his old partner found themselves, just as at their first outset in life, alone. But their family worship continued as of old. At last his fellow traveller left him. Still he carried on the family worship by himself. So sweet was the memory of it in his father's house, and so pleasant had he found it in his own, that he could not give it up. But as he sat in his silent habitation, morning and evening, his quivering voice was overheard singing the old psalm-tune, reading aloud the chapter, and praying as if others still worshipped by his side. He had not found it dull.

"I have no time." If you really value time, family prayer is good husbandry of time. What you do with God's blessing is much better and faster done, than what you do without it, *and is not so likely to need doing over again.* You will find it here as Sir Matthew Hale found it with the Sabbath. What you take from God, he can easily take from you. If other things were equal, I should expect far more to be accomplished in a day, by the man whose spirit had been tranquillized, his resolution fortified, and his activity quickened by morning prayer, than from the man who impiously hurried out to do it all without asking God's presence. Philip Henry, who was an excellent economist of time, when early out of bed to hasten the preparations for a day's travel, as he called his children together, used to say to them, "Prayer and provender hinder no man's journey." Try his homely maxim and you will find it true.

"Our family is so small." How many are there of you? Are there two? Then, "Wheresoever *two*," (see Matt. xviii. 19, 20.) John Howard and his valet, as they journeyed from place, used to have family worship by themselves, if they could get no one else to join them. "Wherever I have a tent," he would say, "there God shall have an altar." If there be two of you—though it should be but a Ruth and a Naomi, a mother and her daughter, your family is large enough to worship God, and to get the blessing of those who worship him.

"My family is so large. There are so many servants, and often so many visiters, that I have not courage to begin." If your family be large, the obligation to begin is all the greater. Many suffer by your neglect. And if your congregation be numerous, the likelihood that some good will be done is the greater; for there are more to share the benefit. And why want courage? Should not the very fact that you are acknowledging God encourage you? "Them that honour me, I will honour." Begin it believingly, and in the very attempt courage will come.

"But I have no gift of prayer. I cannot lead the devotions of my family." Prayer is the gift of the Holy Spirit.* Before you begin, ask God to give you his Spirit to teach you.† I have heard of stammering men who were eloquent in prayer, for the Spirit of God spake by them. When you pray, remember that God is listening. You have called on him to hearken. You have asked him to lend you an attentive ear, for you are about to ask mercies for yourself and your dearest friends. Remember that God is listening, and you will forget that men are hearkening. And they in their turn when they find that you are really praying, will have no time to criticise—for they will be constrained to join you in your prayer.

But perhaps I have not after all touched your real objection. You refuse to pray in your family, because you know that you do not pray in your closet. You evade it, because you know that your life is such that family worship would, in your case, be a mockery, and would only add hypocrisy to sin. Or you are under the influence of that false shame which will be felt to be the most shameful of all things, when the now affronted Son of God comes again in his glory.‡ Is it so? And are you about to throw away this tract with your purpose un-

* Rom. viii. 26. † Luke xi. 13. ‡ Mark viii. 38.

changed? Then I can only say, that the day is coming, when you will wish that you never had any brethren (Luke xvi. 27)—that the Lord had written you childless—that you had been a poor outcast with no roof to shelter you, rather than the ungodly husband and father and master, which you this day are—for then you had been free from blood-guiltiness in the case of others' souls.

The considerations by which I have tried to urge you to a discharge of this duty are, the obligations which you owe to yourselves, to your children, and to God: to yourselves, who will never have the same inward happiness, nor the same satisfaction in your family circle, till once the voice of rejoicing, the melody and praise which are heard in the tabernacles of the righteous, be heard in your own: to your children, who will rise up and call you blessed, if you guide their feet into the way of peace: to God, who offers to become the never slumbering keeper of you and yours, and to uphold your going out and coming in from this time forth for ever. These are the considerations I have used. Some of you may think that I would have succeeded better if I had dwelt on the beautiful and picturesque of family religion; if I had carried you back to the time when the glory of domestic piety had her habitation in our land, when villages and towns presented a look of Sabbath quietness at the hour of morning prayer, and when night succeeding night repeated the praises of God from the lonely upland cottage, to the hamlet on the plain. I might have done this; and I might have planted you amidst the wor shipping household, and invited you to listen to the cordial music of their psalm, and the pathos and fervour of their prayer. But one thing hinders me. I know that all that is beautiful and picturesque in domestic devotion, has not only been witnessed but described by those whom its loveliness could never win to an imitation. It is one thing for a heart full of sensibility to be touched by contemplating the beauty and the joys of true devotion, and quite another thing for a renewed heart to feel these joys. Hundreds have been melted by the matchless poem, in which the bard of Scotland describes the worship of a cottage patriarch; but the *Cottar's Saturday Night* never taught any man to pray. It is told of Sir Walter Scott, that sometimes of an evening he took his guests to an arbour on his lawn, and let them hear the distant music of a sacred tune. It came from the cottage of one of his dependents, and fell touchingly on the ear of the great minstrel himself—but it only touched the ear. He and his visiters went back to the drawing-room at Abbotsford, but it was not to raise with their better skill an evening hymn of thanksgiving to the God of all their mercies. The distant cadence of a covenanting melody was somewhat romantic, but nearer hand it would have blended ill with the dance and the tabret. They all agreed that the voice of psalms from a cottage was picturesque—but that in the mansion, the harp and the viol would be more appropriate.* If higher considerations have no weight, I am sure that a little picture work will not prevail upon you.

Fathers and brethren, some of you are the heads of happy families to-day. All that I ask is, that you would make them happier still—happy, not only in your love, but in the love of God the Saviour, happy for time and through eternity. The happiest family will not be always so. The most smiling circle will be in tears some day. All that I ask is, that you would secure for yourselves and your children, a friend in that blessed Redeemer, who will wipe all tears from all

* These merry halls were soon after silent, and "the voice of harpers, and musicians, and of pipers," has never since been heard in them. The "psalm-singing" servant was a brother born for adversity, and on the breaking-up of the establishment, refused to leave his master, and rather than leave him offered to serve for nothing. In his new post of ploughman, it affected the poor Baronet to hear "Old Peep" whistling to his team, as he trod the fresh-turned furrows. It was a change to both; but it would seem that the one possessed a source of perennial joy which outward calamities could not dry up nor trouble. And after all, in an angel's eye, which is the greater genius—the sublimer spirit—the poet on his Pegasus, or the peasant, who in the hour of calamity can take the wings of a dove, and fly away and be at *rest?* Who that has read the latter days of Robert Burns, does not wish that he had been his own *Cottar?* He sometimes wished it himself. The son of Bosor is not the only man whom the sight of Jacob's goodly tents has made to sigh, "Let me die the death of the righteous."

faces. Your families may soon be scattered, and familiar voices may cease to echo within your walls. They may go each to his own, and some of them may go far away. O see to it, that the God of Bethel goes with them, that they set up an altar, even on a distant shore, and sing the Lord's song in that foreign land. They may be taken from this earth altogether, and leave you alone. O see to it, that as one after another goes, it may be to their Father's house above, and to sing with heavenly voices, and to a heavenly harp, the song which they first learned from you, and with you often sang together here —the song of Moses and the Lamb. And if you be taken, and some of them be left, see to it that you leave them the thankful assurance that you are gone to their Father, and your Father, their God, and your God. And, in the meanwhile, let your united worship be so frequent and so fervent, that when you are taken from their head, the one whose sad office it is to supply your place, as priest of that household, shall not be able to select a chapter or a psalm, with which your living image and voice are not associated, and in which you, though dead, are not yet speaking to them. And thus my heart's wish for you all,

When soon or late you reach that coast,
O'er life's rough ocean driven;
May you rejoice, no wanderer lost,
A family in heaven.

National Scotch Church, Regent-square,
January 1st, 1842.

EXTRACT FROM "THOUGHTS ON FAMILY WORSHIP," BY THE REV. JAMES W. ALEXANDER, OF NEW YORK, PUBLISHED BY THE PRESBYTERIAN BOARD OF PUBLICATION.

Every portion of what has preceded has tended to the single point of inducing the reader to maintain the worship of God in his house, but it is desirable to make the appeal even more closely, and as it were personally, to the heart and conscience. Laying aside, therefore, all more ceremonious modes of approach, I would respectfully and affectionately address myself to the individual professor of religion.

You are, by Providence, set at the head of a family, to support it, instruct it, guard it, and in every way care for its temporal and eternal good. We offer to you a simple means of contributing to the greatest of these objects; and we have, at some length, dwelt upon its excellencies and fruits. Our plea is for those whom you love the best, for your own flesh and blood. No human language can well go beyond the importance of the domestic relation. On this point you require no prompting. When you return from the toils and distractions of the day, and sit at home, amidst the little quiet circle, you feel that you are among your chief wealth. This is your treasure. The law makes it your castle, and religion may make it your sanctuary. As your eye rests on the wife of your bosom, and the pledges of your mutual love, you silently give thanks to God, and sometimes your heart overflows in earnest wishes for the good of each beloved object. Withhold not a single defence or ornament from that Christian home, which is already the source of so many virtues and enjoyments.

> "Domestic happiness, thou only bliss
> Of Paradise that has survived the fall!
> Though few now taste thee unimpaired and pure,
> Or tasting, long enjoy thee! too infirm,
> Or too incautious, to preserve thy sweets
> Unmixed with drops of bitter, which neglect
> Or temper sheds into thy crystal cup;
> Thou art the nurse of Virtue, in thine arms
> She smiles, appearing, as in truth she is,
> Heaven-born, and destined to the skies again." *

If you would "preserve these sweets," connect them with heaven. Have you no desire to honour God, in the midst of these his favours? Or do you see no seemliness in recognising the religion of Christ *in your family capacity?* Even supposing that there were no injunction of such a service as this, one might expect it to grow up spontaneously in Christian households. Prayer is a duty of natural religion. The Mohammedan, wherever he journeys, prays to God five times a day, at his stated hours. The

* Cowper.

very heathen, in their families, call on their gods, "which are yet no gods."* Shall a Christian house be void of all tokens of its relation to God? One might claim of you, as a follower of the Redeemer, to hold forth some such sign, that as for you and your house, you fear the Lord.† If God had given no indications of his good pleasure in this ordinance, it is one of so great value and blessedness, that we might all reasonably join in asking it at his hands as a special boon. But he gives it to us freely; and yet the heavenly gift is spurned by thousands! Suppose it were revealed to us that we were forbidden to worship God in our families! Though all other means should remain undiminished, it would be a fearful interdict; a portentous curfew to our domestic fires. The parent and the child could no longer press around the feet of divine mercy, clinging the more closely because the rest of the world is shut out. Yet multitudes deny themselves all this blessing, of their own free choice; and parents and children grow up and live, and separate, and appear in judgment, without having ever met, even once, in an act of common household supplication. It is amazing, and all but incredible, that any man who loves Christ, should be willing to preside over a family in which, from year to year, there is nothing to signalize it as belonging to the Lord.

* Jeremiah ii. 11. † Joshua xxiv. 15.

O Christian parent! "suffer the word of exhortation." Be persuaded not to deny yourself a service which will heighten all your comforts. The principle is undoubted, that we have tenfold pleasure in that which we enjoy in company with those whom we love. That is not a father's heart, which does not experience it every day. We realize it in our common meals, our recreations, our readings, our excursions, our visits; why should you not realize it in your religion? Family Worship is a coming to God, not singly, but hand-in-hand with your children and family; and from this, its peculiar aspect, it has delights and advantages which are all its own.

The family, as such, has its wants and dangers, and sorrows and sins, which it is, therefore, reasonable to lay before God in a special devotion. No human community stands out from the mass in such substantive and prominent individuality. The circle which bounds it is clear, and sharply marked, and has been described by the hand of God himself. There is a community of interest: no persons on earth are so much bound together. Nothing can befall any one, without reaching the whole circle. You are invited to present your household, as a household, before the infinite Giver of all good. Be assured he will make a difference between those who fear him, and those who fear him not. It was with a dreadful reference to this very family-tie, that God said, "Them that honour me I will honour, and they that despise me shall be lightly esteemed."* Your habitation will be more safe, and its inmates more prosperous, by reason of God's answer to the petitions which you put up together.

* 1 Samuel ii. 30.

THE END.

THE

GOVERNMENT

OF THE THOUGHTS.

BY THE

REV. HENRY FORSTER BURDER, D.D.

PHILADELPHIA:
PRESBYTERIAN BOARD OF PUBLICATION.

THE

GOVERNMENT

OF THE THOUGHTS.

As the right regulation of the thoughts enters deeply and essentially into the nature of personal holiness and happiness, it is important to consider,

First, The importance of the right government of the thoughts; and,

Secondly, The most effectual means of securing this important object.

First, Let me direct your regard to the importance of acquiring and maintaining the due government of the thoughts.

First, then, let it be considered, that the absence of good thoughts is itself a sufficient ground of condemnation at the bar of God.

Of the unrighteous and unholy it is said, "God is not in all their thoughts:" and is not this ample evidence of the prevailing character of their minds and hearts? Must it not be a "carnal mind," and must it not be a hardened heart, in which the thought of God can find no place? Must not the love of God be altogether absent from that heart which gives no entertainment, no dwelling-place, even to the thought of his character and his claims? Is it possible for a man to love God, and yet spend day after day without cherishing any thoughts of God? What ideas are we to form of the man who spends his days without any grateful recollections of the Divine goodness, without any admiring delight in the Divine perfections, without any solicitude to enjoy the Divine favour, and without any desire to promote the Divine glory? That the love of the blessed God dwells not in his heart, is absolutely certain The God in whose hands his breath is, and in whom are all his springs of existence, and capacity, and enjoyment, he has not glorified, even in thought, or purpose, or desire! Let every one, then, listen to the voice of conscience, while summoned to answer the question,—Is it I, whose mental character, whose prevailing habits of thought, have been thus convicted of a radical and most alarming defect?

Let it be considered,

Secondly, That the human mind, while unrenewed, is habitually disposed to the indulgence of thoughts positively vain and evil.

In every human mind which continues unrenewed, not receiving, because not desiring, the control of the sanctifying Spirit, vain and evil thoughts exert an entire ascendency. Thus it was in the world before the flood;

and the record of human depravity at that early period might be adopted by the historian of the age in which we live: "And God saw that the wickedness of man was great in the earth, and that every imagination of the thoughts of his heart was only evil continually." It is to the heart that the scrutinizing and all-pervading eye of the omniscient God is chiefly directed. "The Lord searcheth all hearts, and understandeth all the imaginations of the thoughts." "Man looketh on the outward appearance," and the reason is sufficiently clear; he cannot look beyond. He can form his judgment only by external indications. The man of most profound sagacity can do no more. He may mark, with quickness of discernment, the unstudied action, or the casual word, or the expressive eye, or the voiceless lip, which betrays an emotion in part suppressed. He may deduce, by his acuteness of observation, many an inference which may not mislead; and he may obtain, not unfrequently, an insight into character, which he knows how to value, and how to improve. But the observer, although of most penetrating glance, and most commanding intellect, and most deeply versed in the knowledge of human nature, may be, and often is, deceived. It is probable that even the subtle spirit that "deceiveth the whole world," by the ever-varying artifices of seduction, is sometimes himself deceived; and, extensive as must be his knowledge of the human heart, he can have,

I conceive, no power at all of ascertaining its thoughts and feelings, except in so far as they are expressed or betrayed by certain intelligible indications. Omniscience is no attribute of Satan, nor of any being but Jehovah. In language which no creature can appropriate, does the Father of spirits say, "I the Lord search the heart." And he who uttered these words said also, "The heart is deceitful above all things, and desperately wicked: who can know it?" What, then, must the eye of God discern in every unrenewed heart? What must there be presented to the eye of the Omniscient in the compass of one single day, in the interior of an unregenerate mind? Say, or rather think, what has been sometimes the history of your thoughts within the space of a single hour? Of what character were the subjects on which they were employed? Of what nature were the ideas suggested, cherished, pursued? What was their tendency? and had they been embodied in action, or even expressed in words, what would have been the sentiments awakened in the minds of those to whose approbation you attach a value? Consider, then, that your heart was, at the very moment, "naked and open to the sight of Him with whom you have to do."

Let it be observed,

Thirdly, That it is the characteristic of the renewed mind to cherish good thoughts.

"Let the wicked forsake his way, and the unrighteous man his thoughts:" such is the requirement of Him who "waiteth to be gracious, and delighteth in mercy," but who cannot behold impurity of thought without holy and indignant displeasure. What is the repentance required of the man who would become a recipient of forgiving mercy, but a change of mind, of which the very first element is a change of thought? The very first step of the sinner's return to God, is described with equal simplicity and correctness in such words as these: "I thought on my ways, and turned my feet unto thy testimonies." The next gradation of progress may be exhibited in these stronger terms: "I hate vain thoughts, nor can I endure that any longer they should lodge within me." A stage of still greater advancement appears indicated by such expressions as these: "I thought of thy loving-kindness in the midst of thy temple." And if this be regarded as the representation of a state of mind at one particular period, and not a direct assertion in reference to the prevailing habit of thought, we have at least an interesting and characteristic specimen of a mind truly renewed, in those words of the psalmist, "In the multitude of my thoughts within me, thy comforts delight my soul." Oh, this is indeed the language of a spiritual mind; of a heart right with God! Who can estimate the value, who can describe the delight of this spirituality of mind? "They that are after the flesh do mind the things of the flesh; but they that are after the Spirit, the things of the Spirit.

For to be carnally minded is death; but to be spiritually minded is life and peace."

Let it be considered,

Fourthly, That it is in the thoughts of the mind that both dispositions and actions originate.

"As a man thinketh in his heart, so is he" in the course and character of his life. The thoughts of the mind have been justly compared to the blossoms which appear on a tree in the vernal season of the year. Many of these blossoms prematurely fall off; but from those which remain springs all the fruit which the tree yields: so are there many thoughts which transiently occupy the mind, without leaving any permanent trace; but from the thoughts which are cherished and retained spring all the dispositions of the heart, all the words of the lips, and all the actions of the life. It was worthy, then, of the wisest of men, and worthy of the Spirit of wisdom under whose dictation he wrote, most urgently to enforce the safe keeping of the heart: "Keep thy heart with all diligence;" (or, "above all keeping;") "for out of it are the issues of life." There is no member of our body, there is no organ of sensation, there is no faculty of intellect, there is no avenue of feeling, over which it is not important to exercise a watchful care; but more important still is the guardianship of the heart, whence are all the issues of life. Have you studied the history of the inner man? Have you, with the eye of self-inspection, carefully traced the process which commences with a rising thought, and terminates in an important action? Have you watched the influence of the suggestion, the incentive, the anticipation of consequences, the suspense, and the final resolve? If you are familiar with processes such as these, and with the correspondent results, it is unnecessary for me to make any further demand on your mind, with a view to demonstrate the importance of the right government of the thoughts.

Let your attention be now transferred,

Secondly, To the most effectual means of attaining and preserving the due government of the thoughts.

First, There must be the attainment and the exercise of a good conscience.

The conscience is designed to be the keeper of the mind and heart. Its appointed office is that of a sentinel, to guard the avenues of approach, and to sound the alarm at the first advances of an enemy. But never can the conscience of sinful and degenerate man be competent for such an office, unless the disqualifying influence of guilt be removed, by the efficacy of "the blood which cleanseth from all sin." The heart must remain an impure fountain, whence can issue only polluted streams, unless it be purified by the virtue of atoning blood. It is when "the heart is sprinkled from an evil conscience," as it regards the sins which are past, that we are prepared and disposed so to "exercise ourselves as to have always a conscience void of offence towards God and towards man." The serene repose of spirit which arises from faith in the great propitiation, is conducive to the delicate sensibility which recoils from the contact of defilement, even in the images of thought. Let the language of the verse which has been cited remind us, that if it be our desire to guard against the intrusion of vain and evil thoughts, our hearts must be cleansed from the guilt and pollution of sin. "Wash thine heart from wickedness, that thou mayest be saved. How long shall thy vain thoughts lodge within thee?"

Secondly, The mind must habitually derive from the word of God its best materials of thought.

"I hate vain thoughts," said the psalmist, "but thy law do I love." He knew too much of the tendencies of his own mind, and too much of the universal laws of intellectual being, to wish that the expulsion of vain thoughts should be followed by an uninteresting vacuity of thought. This, were it possible, would be undesirable. It would be a dull and dreary blank in existence. It would be, in the lowest sense, existence; it would not deserve the name of life. But the desire of the man after God's own heart was, that the place vacated by thoughts which were vain, might be filled by thoughts of substantial excellence. This is indeed the best and the only preservative from thoughts decidedly evil. Could the mind be rendered simply vacant, soon would the tempter pour in a strong and rapid tide of his own impure suggestions. The absence of thoughts which are good he regards as the state most favourable to the entrance of thoughts which are evil; so that without any perversion of the meaning of Scripture, we may apply to such a state of mind our Saviour's description of the inducements presented to the evil spirit, to occupy the residence into which he anticipates an unresisting facility of admission: "When the unclean spirit is gone out of a man, he wandereth over parched deserts in search of a resting place.* And not finding any, he saith, I will return to my house whence I came, and being come, he findeth it empty, swept and furnished;" (as if it directly invited his entrance, and was even prepared for his occupation;) "whereupon he goeth and bringeth with him seven other spirits, more wicked than himself; and having entered, there they dwell." "The heart," says an eloquent preacher, "will not consent to be desolated. Though the room which is in it may change one inmate for another, it cannot be left void, without the pain of most intolerable suffering. It could not bear to be left in a state of waste and cheerless insipidity. It would revolt against its own emptiness. Such is the grasping tendency of the human heart, that it must have a something to lay hold of, and which, if wrested away without the substitution of another something in its

* Dr. Campbell's Translation.

place, would leave a void and a vacancy as painful to the mind, as hunger is to the natural system. It may be dispossessed of one object, but it cannot be desolated of all. A man will no more consent to the misery of being without an object, because that object is a trifle, or of being without a pursuit, because that pursuit terminates in some frivolous or fugitive acquirement, than he will voluntarily submit himself to the torture, because that torture is to be of short duration." *

How much of wisdom, then, was there in the method resorted to by the psalmist, with a view to the right government of his thoughts; and how exquisite is the beauty of expression, with which he has described the intellectual and devotional habits of his mind, in the hundred and thirty-ninth Psalm;—"How precious are thy thoughts unto me, O God! how great is the sum of them!" Let us pause a moment, before we proceed to the verse which follows. What can present such admirable and delightful materials, to occupy the thoughts of man, as the book which contains the thoughts of God? Might not the Bible be entitled,—"The Thoughts of God?" Is it not replete with the contemplations of the Eternal Mind? And what are the lofty and the glorious subjects which they present to our regard? They are the attributes of his own nature; the laws which

* Dr. Chalmers.

take their origin from his own rectitude the purposes of mercy emanating from his own love, and extending to rebels against his throne; the mediatorial scheme of redemption, illustrating, in full-orbed glory, the perfections of his own adorable character; the revelations of a future and eternal world of blessedness! Having obtained on these subjects (though less clearly and less fully than we of the gospel-day) the thoughts of God, we wonder not that the psalmist should have exclaimed,—"How precious also are thy thoughts unto me, O God! how great is the sum of them! If I should count them, they are more in number than the sand: when I awake, I am still with thee!" With the thoughts and counsels of Jehovah in his mind, "he lay down at night to rest, and when he awoke in the morning, his thoughts naturally recurred to the pleasing theme; he began where he had left off, and found himself in heart and soul still present with God, still ruminating on him and his works. The mercies of Heaven, in the redemption of the church, by the sufferings and exaltation of the true David—how precious are they to believers! How great is the sum, how far exceeding all human arithmetic to number them! Let them be to us the constant subjects of contemplation, admiration, and thanksgiving, day and night; and let death find us engaged in an employment, which, when we awake, and arise from the grave, we shall resume and prosecute to eternity, in the presence of God!"*

Thirdly, There must be earnest prayer, that our thoughts may be guided and controlled by the influences of the Holy Spirit. "When He, the Spirit of truth, is come," said Jesus to his disciples, "he shall teach you all things, and bring all things to your remembrance, whatsoever I have said unto you." Now, the acquisition of knowledge, and the habitual remembrance of that which is acquired, are usually the result of those two leading operations of the intellect, on which the character of the thoughts chiefly depends. Consider, then, O believer in Jesus, how much you are authorized to expect, in relation to the right government of the thoughts, from the influence so faithfully promised. When you take up the Bible, and read some selected paragraphs, or a chapter in regular course, "the Spirit of wisdom and revelation" can steadily fix your thoughts (too often apt to wander) on some truths of vital importance: he can extend, and correct, and elevate your views, and deepen your impressions of those truths which you knew but imperfectly before; he can give a new direction and a wider range to your ideas, and a new and glowing impulse to the best affections of your hearts. When, at the next return of the hour of retired devotion, you resume the study of the sacred book, some other truths, of no inferior

* Bishop Horne's Commentary.

interest, may be similarly unfolded to your view, and rendered equally influential in awakening the purest affections of the soul. Suppose this to be the history of every day; and suppose the truth into which you have been thus guided, in the commencement of every day, to be held in remembrance throughout the course of the day; will there not be acquired more and more of an invaluable facility in the right government of the thoughts? And is the expectation of this extravagant, or unreasonable? Is it too lofty an expectation for a mind which has already become a temple of the Holy Spirit? And "know ye not that" (if Christians) "ye are the temple of God, and that the Spirit of God dwelleth in you?" Will not, then, the very consideration of the character and influence of the Divine inhabitant, become an incentive to purity of thought? Surely vain thoughts cannot be permitted or tolerated in the temple of the indwelling Deity! Let there be poured forth, then, in importunate prayer, the most fervent petitions, that "the thoughts of the heart may be cleansed by the inspiration of the Holy Spirit."

Fourthly, There must be the diligent culture of all holy affections.

While it is true, that the thoughts give excitement to the affections, it is equally true, that the affections give excitement to the thoughts. The affections are the wings on which the intellect itself is sustained, in the soaring elevation of its flight, above the regions of sense. Even in the pursuits of literature and of science, it would be vain to expect a rapid or a pleasurable progress, without the stimulus arising from a predilection of taste, and a feeling of powerful attachment. How much more is that incentive required in the application of the mind to subjects decidedly spiritual! Would you, then, acquire an aptitude for the employment of the thoughts on things unseen and eternal? Would you obtain an increasing degree of facility, in disengaging the powers of thought from all earth-sprung cares and entanglements? Would you rise, as on the wings of eagles, to a region more pure and serene, that you may contemplate, in an unclouded atmosphere, "the things which are above?" Be it your solicitous care to "keep your hearts in the love of God," by "praying in the Holy Ghost." Be assured, that when most deeply "rooted and grounded in love," you will be able to put forth the best energies of your minds, in endeavouring to comprehend what is the breadth, and length, and depth, and height; and to know the love of Christ, which passeth knowledge!

Fifthly, We must habitually realize the Divine inspection of our thoughts.

Suppose that your unexpressed and most secret thoughts could be ascertained by a fellow creature, as soon as they found a place in your mind. Suppose that some one individual had certain means of knowing your thoughts, over which you could exercise nc control, what emotions would you feel in his presence! What intense anxiety would you betray, as well as feel, to repress the very first rising of thoughts, which you might deem unworthy of your character, and, in his estimation, disgraceful! But are not you, at every moment, and in every situation, whether acting, or speaking, or thinking, under the inspection of an omniscient and omnipresent eye? And is it not with Him, as "the Judge of all," that, in a sense inapplicable to any human observer, "you have especially to do?" Let, then, the emphatic words of Hagar dwell for ever in "the imagination of the thoughts of your hearts"—"Thou, God, seest me!" Enter deeply into the spirit which regulated the thoughts of the psalmist:—"O Lord, thou hast searched me, and known me. Thou knowest my down-sitting, and mine up-rising, thou understandest my thoughts afar off. Thou compassest my path and my lying down, and art acquainted with all my ways."

Lastly, It is requisite that we frequently take a retrospect of the history of our thoughts, for the purpose of self examination.

With unfeigned sincerity may we say to Him, who knows the recesses of our hearts, far better than than we know them ourselves, "Search me, O God, and know my heart: try me, and know my thoughts: and see" (and enable me to see) "if there be any wicked way in me, and lead me in the way everlasting." Awfully hypocritical would it be to offer these petitions, without the most determined efforts of scrutinizing self inspection. At the close of every day, and still more strenuously at the close of every ampler period of our time, let us call ourselves to render an account of the employment of our thoughts. Let the detection of evil thoughts produce its proper and legitimate effects. Let it humble us in the dust of abasement; let it conduct us to the cross of the Redeemer; let it rouse us to greater watchfulness in guarding against the intrusion of vain and evil thoughts; and let it urge us to more earnest prayer that the God of all grace would effectually control and sanctify the thoughts of our hearts, by "working in us all the good pleasure of his goodness, and the work of faith with power."

In conclusion, let me suggest the inquiry, whether the considerations which have been adduced, ought not to excite in the minds of some who have thought but little on the subject, serious misgivings and apprehensions, with regard to their character in the sight of God. Does not conscience, at this moment, bring against you a most appalling charge? Does it not charge you with innumerable iniquities of thought? Does it not charge you with the additional guilt of thinking lightly of those iniquities? You cannot deny, that sins of thought are the very spring and fountain of sins in conduct. You cannot deny, that many of your sinful thoughts have been rapidly maturing into principles of action, and have wanted only the force of a besetting temptation to bring them into practical development. You cannot deny, that among the countless multitude of thoughts, which have crowded the entire space between the morning and the evening of many a day, there have been instances in which not one single thought of God, of Christ, or of eternity, obtained admission. Yet is it not specified, as one of the decided characteristics of those who are unfit for heaven, and exposed to endless woe, that "God is not in all their thoughts?" And is it not expressly said, by the authority of Him who searcheth the heart, that "the wicked shall be turned into hell, and all the nations" (and therefore all the individuals) "that forget God?" Oh, what must be the accumulation of the guilt contracted, if, with respect to sins of thought alone, a charge can be substantiated, of a nature sufficiently heinous in the sight of God to require a sentence of eternal banishment from his presence! Hasten, then, to his throne of grace, lest he summon thee, at an unexpected hour, to his throne of judgment! Supplicate, in the name of the only Saviour, deliverance from the wrath to come! Pray that the thoughts of thine heart, as well as the sins of thy life, may be forgiven thee. And, oh, what an inducement to offer that prayer, is the assurance, that, with the God whom thou hast insulted and forgotten, "there is forgiveness!"—"Let the wicked forsake his way, and the unrighteous man his thoughts: and let him return unto the Lord, and he will have mercy upon him; and to our God, for he will abundantly pardon." Let those vain thoughts be for ever abandoned, which fostered vain hopes, and delusive expectations.

No longer expose to final condemnation your immortal soul, by trusting in yourselves, as though you were righteous, or by neglecting to seek an interest, by faith, in the righteousness of Jesus. Never let it be absent from your minds, that "he was made sin for us, though he knew no sin, that we might be made the righteousness of God in him." Let, then, "the word of Christ,"—the glorious gospel which bringeth salvation,—"dwell in you richly, in all wisdom and spiritual understanding." Let it be the purifier of your heart, the regulator of your thoughts. Let the treasures of Divine truth be amply stored within your hearts, and let them be employed as the materials of pleasurable thought, "when you are sitting in the house, and when you are walking by the way, and when you are lying down, and when you are rising up." Then will "the peace of God which passeth all understanding, keep your hearts and minds through Christ Jesus;" to whom be glory for ever. Amen.

THE

GOVERNMENT

OF THE TONGUE.

BY THE

REV. HENRY FORSTER BURDER, D.D.

PHILADELPHIA:
PRESBYTERIAN BOARD OF PUBLICATION.

THE

GOVERNMENT

OF THE TONGUE.

"THE tongue," affirms the apostle, "can no man tame." Animals the most fierce and the most formidable have been subjected to the rule of man, and by his sagacity, rendered tractable and docile. But it transcends all human power to impose an effectual curb on the tongue of unregenerate man, or entirely to counteract the venom emitted from his lips. Hopeless, however, as might be the effort to control the tongue of another, not so is the attempt to control our own. It is confessedly difficult, but it is indispensably requisite: for the same apostle has said, "If any man among you seem to be religious, and bridleth not his tongue, but deceiveth his own heart, this man's religion is vain." The government of the tongue, then, it is absolutely necessary to attain; and he who acquires it in the highest degree, is the Christian of most distinguished eminence:—"If any man offend not in word, the same is a perfect man, and able also to bridle the whole body." The human body is here represented, by the apostle, as a complex system of members and organs, designed to be subject to the authority, and subservient to the purposes of the indwelling mind. Of these organs there is one, over which it is peculiarly difficult to obtain a due ascendency. If then that control be acquired, much easier will be the task of duly restraining the rest; so that the man who has acquired the government of his tongue, may be supposed to have attained a correspondent dominion over all the organs, over all the senses, and over all the appetites of the corporeal frame. If any man, therefore, could be found, who, since the acquisition of that power, had never in any instance abused, or failed to improve, the faculty of speech, he might be regarded as a perfect man: and, in so far as there is an approach to this exalted attainment, there is acquired, by the controlling mind, a facility in bridling and governing the complex system of "the outward man."

Let me, then, engage your attention,

First, To the peculiar importance of the government of the tongue; and,

Secondly, To the principles by which this government is to be acquired and maintained.

First, Let us reflect on the importance of attaining this control.

First, Consider the dignity and excellence of the faculty of speech.

He who delights to gather materials for admiration and praise, out of the curious and wondrous economy of man's living frame, will find much to repay his researches in the contemplation of the faculty of speech. Think of the delicate and difficult articulation which intelligible speech requires. Think of the combination of a few simple and elementary sounds, denoted by a small number of alphabetical characters, so as to form all the thousands of words which we employ in the conveyance of thought. Think of the power acquired in early life, of connecting with these sounds the ideas which they are employed to express; so that even before the formalities of education have commenced, there has been an admirable progress made in the knowledge of the arbitrary symbols of thought, by means of which we converse. Think of the power of memory which the use of language involves. Think of the influence of words in aiding and guiding all our processes of thought, even when no sentence escapes our lips. Who gave us this power of articulate speech, which raises us so far above the most sagacious of all the inferior tribes of animated nature? Who sustains all the delicate sensibilities of the ear and of the tongue, required for distinct articulation? Answer such questions as these, and surely you will not be disposed to unite with those who say, "Our tongues are our own; who is Lord over us?" Surely, if you feel aright, you will enter into the grateful emotions of him who exclaimed, "Awake up, my glory: my heart is prepared; I will sing and give praise, even with my glory."

Secondly, Consider the influence which the tongue is capable of exerting over the minds and characters of others.

Can you specify the country, or the age, or the condition of society, in which this influence has not been powerful? Conceive of the effects produced, even on a tribe of savages, by the simple and vehement oratory of a warlike chief. Conceive, if you are able, of the effects produced on a democratic assembly of ancient Greeks by the energies of Demosthenian eloquence. You have sometimes felt, perhaps, the willing subjugation of the soul to the fascinating and commanding talents of some master of the power of speech, who knew well the avenues which give access to the human heart. And long before it was possible for you to know what the word eloquence denotes, you felt the power of the living, and animating, and soothing voice. You listened to the music of a mother's most endearing accents, and to the joy-inspiring tones of a father's voice of love. And as your capabilities of thought began to unfold themselves under parental fosterage, you imbibed full many a sentiment, and received full many an impression, even while you were only in the act of acquiring the use of your mother tongue. And what is the history of all your companionship, but the history of the reciprocal influences of thought and feeling, communicated through the medium of speech? The influence which in your early days you felt, without tracing it to its source, you have long since begun to exert, and you are daily in the habit of exerting, over the minds of those around you. Is that influence,—let me most earnestly and affectionately inquire,—is that influence of a character beneficial, or is it of a character injurious to the dearest interests of your associates? Would they have been losers, or would they have been gainers, had they never listened to your voice?

Thirdly, Consider the awful responsibility connected with the employment of the tongue.

Hear the declaration of Him who will hereafter occupy that throne, before which shall be gathered all nations: "I say unto you, that every idle word that men shall speak, they shall give account thereof in the day of judgment. For by thy words thou shalt be justified, and by thy words thou shalt be condemned." It is, I conceive, as if our Lord had said: "The evidences of thy character shall be sufficiently gathered from the words of thy lips; so that, independently of thine actions, there will be abundant materials for the decisions of the judgment-day." Even a philosophic heathen could say, "Such as a man is, such are his words:" and He who knew, infinitely better, what is in man, said, "Out of the abundance of the heart the mouth speaketh." If the tongue, in one single conversation, or even in one significant expression, may be regarded as the index to the heart, what a mass of materials for the proceedings of the judgment-seat must be accumulating every day of life, as the words, whether thoughtfully or heedlessly, are falling from our lips! What an awakening consideration should it at all times prove,—that every word we speak is heard by Him whose ear (no less than his eye) is in every place; and that every utterance of the lips is recorded in "the book of His remembrance!" Oh for the blotting out, then, of "the handwriting that is against us" in that book! Oh for an interest in the abundant mercy of Him who has said, "I, even I, am He that blotteth out thy transgressions for mine own sake, and will not remember thy sins!" Who that attempts to retrace the history of the communications of his own lips, will not acknowledge the necessity of an interest in the sacrifice of expiation which was offered on Calvary? What can authorize the feeling of repose and tranquillity in the prospect of the day of account, but a believing reliance on the mercy of God through our Lord Jesus Christ, who was "made sin for us," though he "knew no sin, that we might be made the righteousness of God in him?"

No doubt, then, it may be presumed, can remain on your minds, with regard to the peculiar and inexpressible importance of the government of the tongue. You are prepared, I trust, to direct your willing attention,

Secondly, To the principles on which we should aim at acquiring that control.

First, Let our chief anxiety be directed to the fountain of thought and of language.

Hopeless will be the effort to purify the streams, unless the source be pure. Unreasonable will be the expectation of valuable fruit, unless the tree be good. In the discourse of our Saviour, to which I have already adverted, this subject is placed in the clearest and the strongest light. "Either make the tree good, and his fruit good; or else make the tree corrupt, and his fruit corrupt: for the tree is known by his fruit.—How can ye, being evil, speak good things?—A good man out of the good treasure of the heart bringeth forth good things: and an evil man out of the evil treasure bringeth forth evil things." Who, then, is the good man, whose heart contains a good treasure of the materials requisite for edifying discourse? It is the man who is prepared to speak of God, and of Christ, and of heaven, because he delights to think of God, and of Christ, and of heaven. It is the man who is "spiritually-minded," being "born of the Spirit," and "led by the Spirit," as one of "the children of God." Wonder not, then, that it should have been said by the Saviour, "Ye must be born again."

To those who have the hope and the evidence of this renewal of the mind, I would say:—Let the keeping of the heart be the care of every day. Let it be right with God and let it be right with man. Let the love of God dwell there, and it will be your delight, with your lips, "to bless his name, abundantly to utter the memory of his great goodness, to speak of the glory of his kingdom, to make known his mighty acts, to testify of his righteousness, and to show forth his salvation." Let that love of man, also, which thinketh no evil, dwell there, and evil-speaking will, in no instance, defile your lips. From those lips shall ever flow the words of kindness, because the law of love is written on the heart.

Secondly, Let us avoid and detest all those abuses of the tongue by which the power of speech would be perverted, and its utility counteracted.

These abuses include—

1. All that is inconsistent with truth.

He who asserts a falsehood, or promotes deception, or violates the confidence reposed in him for veracity, does what in him lies to destroy all the securities of society, to undermine the very basis of its constitution, and to reduce it to a state of pitiable and wretched barbarism. If even among men of the world every species of untruth is considered despicable and degrading, oh how high should be the standard of veracity and sincerity among the disciples of that Divine Master, "in whose lips was found no guile!' "Speak ye every one truth to his neighbour;" —truth without subterfuge, and without equivocation; truth which will bear the scrutiny of conscience; yes, and of that Searcher of the heart, "whose eyes are as a flame of fire."

These abuses include—

2. All that is inconsistent with the feelings of Christian kindness and charity.

On this head I offer, without apology, the forcible and pungent remarks of Dr. Chalmers:—"It is a fault to speak evil one of another, but the essence of the fault lies in the want of that charity which thinketh no evil. Had the heart been filled with this principle, no such bad thing as slander would have come out of it. The forms of evil speaking, however, break out into manifold varieties. There is the resentful outcry. There is the manly and indignant disapproval. There is the invective of vulgar malignity. There is the poignancy of satirical remark. There is the giddiness of mere volatility, which spreads its entertaining levities over a gay and light-hearted party. These are all so many transgressions of one and the same duty: and you can easily conceive an enlightened Christian sitting in judgment over them all, and taking hold of the right principle upon which he would condemn them all; and which, if brought to bear with efficacy on the consciences of the different offenders, would not merely silence the passionate evil-speaker out of his outrageous exclamations, and restrain the malignant evil-speaker from his deliberate thrusts at the reputation of the absent; but would rebuke the humorous evil-speaker out of his fanciful and amusing sketches, and the gossiping evil-speaker out of his tiresome and never-ending-narratives."

To this vivid and pointed specification by the Christian preacher, allow me to add a sentence or two from the pen of a French moralist; appealing, it is confessed, to principles of an inferior order, yet such as are well calculated to produce effect:—"He of whom you delight to speak evil, may become acquainted with what you have said, and he will be your enemy: or, if he remain in ignorance of it, you will still have to reproach yourself with the meanness of attacking one who had no opportunity of defending himself. If scandal is to be secret, it is the crime of a coward; if it is to become known, it is the crime of a madman."

The abuses to be avoided include—

3. All that is inconsistent with the utmost delicacy and purity.

Hear the inspired writer of the epistle to the Ephesians: "Let no corrupt communication proceed out of your mouth,—neither filthiness, nor foolish talking, nor jesting, which are not convenient:" or, rather, which are not to be tolerated; being highly offensive to God, and highly injurious to man. From the import of the terms employed in the original, the apostle is supposed to advert here, to artfully turned expressions, in which more is meant than meets the ear, and more than the modest ear could tolerate;—in which, by words of double meaning, there is displayed the execrable wit, that renders terms, in themselves not indelicate, the vehicle, when artfully combined, of conveying ideas indelicate in the highest degree. From uttering and from hearing this language of deep depravity, may the God of all grace preserve the young!

Let these hints suffice, in reference to the many abuses of the tongue, which it is of the greatest importance to avoid.

Thirdly, Let there be more than ordinary vigilance, where there is more than ordinary danger.

Consideration should, in every instance, precede expression. If we would adopt the only rational method in which words can be uttered, we must determine, first to think, and then to speak. "Either be silent," said Pythagoras to his disciples, "or say something that is better than silence." And a greater than Pythagoras has said; "In the multitude of words there wanteth not sin: but he that refraineth his lips is wise." "Seest thou a man that is hasty in his words? there is more hope of a fool than of him." But if the habit of consideration be at all times desirable, how much more requisite must it be in circumstances of peculiar danger!

That danger may arise sometimes from within, and originate in our own hearts Often it may be imminent, under the impulse of strong and ardent feeling, and especially under the excitement of angry and tumultu ous emotions. How important, then, is the exhortation of the apostle James: "Let every man be swift to hear, slow to speak, slow to wrath: for the wrath of man worketh not the righteousness of God." If wrath be rising, if the storm be gathering in thy soul, summon to thine aid the most effectual principles of self-control. Suspect thyself; dread thyself; and look up to Him who is able, in the moment of peril, "to succour them that are tempted."

The danger to be apprehended arises sometimes from without, still more than from within. Of this source of peril the psalmist was feelingly aware:—"I said, I will take heed to my ways, that I sin not with my tongue: I will keep my mouth with a bridle, while the wicked is before me. I was dumb with silence, I held my peace, even from good; and my sorrow was stirred." If, as in the case of David, injuries have been received, there may be danger of uttering, in return, impatient, and impetuous, and resentful, and recriminating, and heart-cutting words. If favours have been received, there may be danger of yielding a sinful assent to the opinions expressed, and the principles maintained. In the hours of social intercourse, how gradual and easy is often the transition from the expression of sentiments with which you may safely accord, to the utterance of sentiments with which it would be culpable to accord; and, under these circumstances, how perplexing and entangling does the course of conversation often become! What a painful and difficult struggle then commences in the mind, between the fear of offending man, and the fear of offending God! And although a holy decision of character will promptly determine in what manner the struggle shall terminate, who is there that cannot perceive the extreme danger of such a situation to the timid, the modest, and the young? Nor let it be forgotten, that silence itself may be sin; and sin it undoubtedly is, if it proceed from that "fear of man which bringeth a snare;" —a fear of boldly avowing the principles of the gospel, and maintaining the honour of the cause of Christ. "Whosoever shall be ashamed of me and of my words," said the Lord Jesus, "of him also shall the Son of man be ashamed, when he cometh in the glory of his Father with the holy angels."

Fourthly, Let us remember, that it is incumbent upon us to conduct our social intercourse, so as not only to avoid doing evil, but also to effect all possible good.

Not satisfied with saying merely, "Let no corrupt communication proceed out of your mouth;" the apostle added, "but that which is good to the use of edifying, that it may minister grace unto the hearers." The Christians of Colosse are also thus exhorted:— "Let your speech be alway with grace, seasoned with salt, that ye may know how ye ought to answer every man." It is as if the apostle had said:—"Let there be in your conversation a principle of holy vitality which may prove that your hearts are alive to God: let there be in it a corrective principle, preventing the tendencies to that which is corrupt,—too often apparent in social intercourse: let there be in it the virtue of a powerful stimulant, exciting the minds of others to all that is pure and salutary, while it imparts to conversation a zest most gratifying to the spiritual taste." And ought we to feel at a loss for materials to conduct, on those principles, the interchange of thought and sentiment, in the hours of friendly intercourse? What was the subject on which the two celestial visitants conversed with our Lord, on the mount which was the scene of his transfiguration? What was the class of subjects on which Jesus usually conversed with his disciples? What were the subjects most interesting to the minds of those primitive Christians, who "continued stedfastly in the apostles' doctrine and fellowship, and in breaking of bread, and in prayers; and they did eat their meat with gladness and singleness of heart, praising God, and having favour with all the people?" No dejection sat on their countenance; no melancholy brooded over their minds; no moroseness could be detected in their demeanour; no insipidity rendered unattractive their conversation; yet we cannot doubt that their chief and favourite topics of discourse were connected with "the decease accomplished at Jerusalem," and its wondrous and glorious results. What other subjects could be in their estimation equally interesting, when, with one mind and one heart they "counted all things but loss for the excellency of the knowledge of Christ Jesus their Lord;" and were chiefly solicitous to live to his glory on earth, and to dwell eternally in his presence in heaven? Oh that we could imbibe more of their spirit, and then it would be easier to imitate, in some degree, the style and character of their heavenly conversation! Were this attained, what incalculable benefits might we not diffuse throughout the sphere of our social intercourse!

Fifthly, Let us connect with our best directed efforts our most earnest prayers for Divine aid.

A most appropriate prayer is to be found in the effusion of the inspired psalmist:—"Lord, I cry unto thee: make haste unto me; give ear unto my voice, when I cry unto thee. Let my prayer be set forth before thee as incense; and the lifting up of my hands as the evening sacrifice. Set a watch, O Lord, before my mouth; keep the door of my lips." Our daily prayers, including petitions such as these, should have, as much as possible, the regularity and the constancy of the morning and the evening sacrifice anciently offered at Jerusalem; and if offered by faith in Him of whose atoning blood those sacrifices were the appointed symbols, they will rise to heaven as accept ably as the cloud of odoriferous and emble matic incense. If we thus lift up our ardent desires to God for communications which He alone can bestow, we shall not fail to receive the aid of heavenly grace, in restraining our lips from evil, and in exciting that spirituality of mind which is the best preparative for the hours of social intercourse. If we habitually converse much with God, we shall have the best preparation for conversing well and profitably with men. It will then also become easy and natural to us to offer such petitions as the psalmist's, not merely in the hours of periodical devotion, but at every moment of solicitude and of danger, when aid from above may be especially required.

Lastly, Let us examine ourselves frequently, at the bar of conscience, in reference to the government of the tongue.

Have we not, on this subject, occasion for very deep regret, and penitential abasement of spirit? How little have we honoured God by the improvement of this noble faculty, his gracious gift! How little have we effected by the power of speech, for the spiritual benefit of those around us! Were we to be deprived of this faculty, in any degree, by the effect of paralyzing disease, how heavy a burden might our consciences feel, from the recollections of our misimprovement of this invaluable gift! Are there not some who, instead of doing good, have occasioned incalculable evil by the abuse of the tongue? "The tongue" of some "is a fire, a world of iniquity: so is the tongue among our members, that it defileth the whole body, and setteth on fire the course of nature; and it is set on fire of hell." So let it not be with any one of us! May pardon be obtained for past offences, and past deficiencies, through the atoning sacrifice of Jesus: and may there be granted, in answer to prayer, the effectual aid of the Holy Spirit to control and sanctify the faculty of speech; that "not offending in word," we may attain the perfection referred to in the passage before quoted, being able to govern, by most effectual discipline, the whole economy of "the outward man," to the glory of our God, and the spiritual and eternal benefit of all within the sphere of our influence.

REMEMBER ELI.

A SOLEMN CALL UPON PARENTS TO REMEMBER THE ACCOUNT WHICH THEY MUST GIVE FOR THEIR CHILDREN'S SOULS.

BY THE REV. R. M. M'CHEYNE.

"His sons made themselves vile, and he restrained them not."—1 SAM. iii. 13.

"And I saw the dead, small and great, stand before God."—REV. xx. 12.

THERE is a report in heaven, as well as among us, that many of you are guilty of your children's blood. It is believed that many of you allow your children to perish miserably. We wish you to inquire whether or not you be really chargeable with this fearful crime.

You know that every minister and elder has a twofold account to give at the judgment-seat of Christ; and so has every father and mother. One of these accounts is to be regarding their own souls; and the other is to be regarding how they attended to those under their care. This last account will be as strict as the first; for one of the holy prophets declares that there is an unutterable woe lying upon those who "feed themselves, and do not feed the flock," Ezekiel xxxiv. 2. Now, parents, you "feed yourselves," and fall under this woe, when you are content with getting meat, and drink, and clothing, while you let your children become a prey to wolves, that is, to wicked companions, bad example, temptations to sinful amusements and pleasure, by which their souls are ruined for ever.

Oh! remember you have to give an account for your own souls! and that will be fearful enough, and sad enough! God will open the great book of judgment, and turn to the page wherein your sins are written. His bright light will shine on the page, and you will be forced to come up the steps of the judgment-seat, and read what is written against you. Your conscience will testify that every word is true; and the devil will be a witness, for he led you into the mire; and holy angels will declare how they saw and shuddered at your sin; and many of your neighbours will be brought up to tell how you and they sinned together; and God himself will speak, and declare it to be all true! Oh! how awful is the prospect! You will, on that day, be damned, if all these things are found in the book! But there is another account even after all this is done, namely, the account you have to give for your children,—for each of your children, and each of their sins! You will be reckoned guilty of their sins, if you did not check them; you will be accounted chargeable with their follies and vices, if you agreed to let them go on in what way they pleased, 1 Sam. iii. 13. And who will be the witness against you here? Will it be conscience, and the devil, and your neighbour, and the Holy God? Yes, but in addition, your own little children! Your own children will face you at the judgment-seat, and condemn you! Alas, their agonized looks,—their tears,—their cries,—their gnashing of teeth, will then awaken your conscience, and you will be proved before the universe to be murderers of your own children's souls!

The mother of a little girl used to teach her to pray, but only at times that suited her own convenience. One day this little girl looked in her mother's face, and said, "Mother, when I die and go to heaven, and God Almighty asks me, 'Did your mother teach you to pray?' I will tell him, 'yes, except on washing days.'" Was not this a case where the child seemed already to be beginning her office as witness against her parent's sin? But there was another girl, whose history was far more awful. She had once cared about her soul, and sought a Saviour, till her father led her away back to the world and its sins. In the course of a year after he had succeeded in making his daughter thoughtless and gay, a rapid fever attacked her. She called for her father in her last moments, fixed her eyes on him, and was able to utter, "Father, last year I would have sought Christ, but now, father, your child is ——." She had not time to finish the sentence, death arrested her! but, oh! what a witness she will be when she meets him again, and reproaches him with having ruined her soul! There is a hymn which has often struck us as being very solemn and alarming,—a hymn that represents lost children upbraiding their parents. They are crying from the lowest hell, telling their parents that if they had taken an interest in their souls, they would never have come into that place of torment.

"Father, weep with shame and rueing,
Weep for thy child's undoing,
For the days when I was young,
And no prayer was taught my tongue—
I ran the world's race well,
And find my portion, Hell!

Weep, mother, weep; but know
'Twill not shorten endless woe!—
Weep my lost spirit's fate,
But know thy tears too late!
Had they sooner fallen—well,
I had not wept in Hell!"

O parents! are any of you already stained with this crimson guilt? Have any of you cause to fear that you have sent some of your children to hell by your conduct? Or have you reason to fear lest you have set them on the way, although they are still alive? Up, and flee to the city of refuge! You are like the ancient man-slayers, (Numbers xxxv.,) the avenger of blood is at your heels! there is no remission for your sin, except in the blood of Jesus. And Jesus has made so full and ample an atonement that, on the ground of it, even a murderer of souls may be forgiven. Manasseh was a murderer of souls, and he was forgiven through this precious blood. (2 Chron. xxxiii.) You, too, may be forgiven, if your blood-stained conscience be washed in the precious blood of the Lamb. Your souls may now be sore vexed, and ill at ease ; your peace may be broken up, and remorse may have well nigh begun that gnawing which shall never end ; but hearken to the words that bring you glad tidings : "The chastisement of our peace was laid upon Him." (Isa. liii. 5.)

We know that if you would bathe in the blood of Him who "his ownself bare our sins, in his own body, on the tree," then would your souls be delivered from the oppressive and intolerable thought of the past, and you would be refreshed in the future, by the glorious prospect of bringing those that remain, to the same Saviour that redeemed you. It is true you may feel like the South Sea murderers of their children, who, on being awakened, and taught the power of the blood of Christ, even then found the consciousness of that sin—the murder of their children—the last which they could bring to his atoning blood. Some lamented in agony over seven, others over seventeen or twenty, whom they had destroyed. Yet even these did at last find their souls cleansed in that full, deep fountain. And you may find the same! You will then be like pardoned Manasseh, who, when justified from all things by bathing in the ocean of Immanuel's blood, could walk at evening round Zion, and look down into the very valley of Hinnom—the black, gloomy valley where he had made so many of his children pass through the fire to Moloch,—and still retain his peace with God, and say, "Who is he that condemneth? It is Christ that died." (Rom. viii. 34.) If you would thus try the power of Christ's sacrifice to purify your guilty conscience, you would soon care for and yearn over your children's souls. You would discover their guilt, and perceive their danger, and you would long to see them saved and made "accepted in the Beloved." We know, also, in regard to those of you that have sought Christ for yourselves, but have not been sufficiently careful to fulfil your baptismal promise, and comply with the demand of the Lord, by bringing your children to Christ; we know that the cause is to be found in your meager views and most inadequate feelings of the Saviour's glorious work. Your sense of the heinousness of the sin which it purges away, is so dull, and your apprehension of its infinitely urgent necessity and overwhelming grace, is so dim, that your languid feelings are not stirred, though your offspring are living in the open neglect of the great salvation. Were you to die in your present unfaithfulness to your family and be saved yourselves, "so as by fire," you would need to take an eternal farewell of your children. Like Eli, you might be saved; but your feelings on reaching glory would be like his. No doubt he learned in heaven what he dreaded to think upon on earth, that his sons, Hophni and Phineas, were cast away as brands for the burning; and now all that he could do, as he stood before the throne—himself saved, but none of his offspring—was first to adore the sovereign grace that had led himself to wash in the blood of the Lamb that removed even that sin of crimson and scarlet dye, and next to join the hallelujahs of the company that were praising the righteous wrath of their God, against the lost souls of Hophni and Phineas, while they saw the smoke of their torments rising up for ever and ever. (Rev. xix. 3.)

Bearing these solemn truths in mind, hear us when we propose to you that your children should be sent to the SABBATH SCHOOL.

I. You that care about your own and your children's souls. We believe you are seeking out the best means of benefitting those under your care. We, therefore, do no more than ask you to consider whether or not it would be useful to send your children to our schools. If other circumstances are suitable, then your example might influence some of your neighbours; and by your attention to your children, in preparing them at home for the Sabbath School, you would have the satisfaction of seeing your children become a pattern to others.

II. You that care about your children, though you are not yourselves converted. We know that this is no uncommon case; even infidels have wished their children to know Christ. Now, if you feel that you yourselves have got no change of heart, we entreat you to send your children to the Sabbath School. There, by the blessing of God, they may be led to Christ. The teacher's whole aim is to bring them to the cross of Christ, to carry them to the Shepherd who gave his life for the sheep, and to bathe them in the fountain open for sin and uncleanness. But if you allow them to spend Sabbath evening, and perhaps all the day too, in whatever manner they please, you may expect soon to hear them uttering oaths, and be grieved by their profanity, their contempt for the ordinances of God, their filthy and foolish deeds, and other signs of a hardened heart. But oh! if they were saved, you would be freed at the great day from the reproach of their ruin. And perhaps they might even carry home salvation to you! What if they should lead you by the hand to Jesus? What if your experience should be that of a parent who said, "I was thirty years old before I knew that I had a soul. But one of our boys went out on a Sabbath to play, and was brought in with his ankle-bone out of joint. Next Sabbath another of the boys got himself lamed. I resolved to send them to school to be out of the way. It was there that they learned, and I learned through them, that I had a soul."

III. You that care neither for your own nor your children's souls. Whether you care or not, still it is true that there is a Saviour standing with open arms, saying, "Suffer little children to come unto me, and forbid them not." (Mark x. 14.) Will you allow us to be kind to them, and lead them to this Saviour? You would wish them to be obedient, to be well behaved, to be useful you would not wish to see them grow up to be thieves, drunkards, and pests to society. Let us, then, do what we can to lead them to Christ. Do not hinder us from showing kindness to your children. We entreat you not to be unmerciful to their souls. Let not your eye be evil toward the children of your own bowels. Would you wish that any of them should yet curse the day that ever they were born in your house, and had you for their parent?

And now that we have ended our few words of expostulation, we must say to those of you who agree to put your children under our care for a few hours on Sabbath, that we do not in any degree free you from the obligations you yourselves are under to attend to their souls. No; we cannot take upon us your responsibility, which became yours at your children's birth, and was sealed on you at their baptism. We cannot stand in your place at the judgment-day. You must yourselves at home watch over them, pray for them and with them, help them in their lessons for their classes, and speak to them on their returning home, as anxiously as if we had never said a word. We offer only to help you. It will prove your more sure condemnation at last, if it be the case that strangers cared more for your children's souls than you yourselves do,—the father that begat them, and the mother that bore them. But, oh! how blessed, if, led by the Holy Spirit yourselves, you become the means of leading your children to Jesus! We will stand by, rejoicing to hear you say, "Behold, Lord, I and the children whom thou hast given me!"

Suffer me to come to Jesus,
  Mother dear, forbid me not;
By his blood from hell he frees us,
  Makes us fair, without a spot.

Suffer me, my earthly father,
  At his pierced feet to fall;
Why forbid me? help me rather;
  Jesus is my all in all.

Suffer me to run unto him;
  Gentle sisters, come with me;
Oh that all I love but knew him,
  Then my home a heaven would be.

Loving playmates, gay and smiling,
  Bid me not forsake the cross;
Hard to bear is your reviling,
  Yet for Jesus all is dross.

Yes, though all the world have chid me,
Father, mother, sister, friend—
Jesus never will forbid me!
Jesus loves me to the end!

Gentle Shepherd, on thy shoulder
Carry me, a sinful lamb;
Give me faith, and make me bolder,
Till with thee in heaven I am.

AN ADDRESS TO PARENTS.

We feel deeply concerned to be useful to the souls of your children; and, no doubt, *you* feel a strong desire that they may be happy; but in order that this may be the case, you must help us to bring them up in the fear of the Lord; that is, you must *pray* for them, and pray with them. If you answer, "I never prayed for myself; how, then, am I to pray for my children?" we ask, how will you, how can you, answer for this awful neglect at the day of judgment? Oh begin at once; begin to-day; kneel down with your child, and say, "Lord, pardon my sins for the sake of Jesus Christ. Create in me a clean heart, O God; and renew a right spirit within me." Pray on in this way till you receive an answer. You must be born again, or die to all eternity. You often feel very unhappy, very angry, and wretched; and you feel so because your heart is wicked, proud, sinful; opposed to God, to holiness, and your own happiness. Now you will never be right till you obtain peace with God through our Lord Jesus Christ.

Again, you must take your children *to the house of God.* Many parents allow their children to run in the streets on the Sabbath, where they hear all manner of bad words, and learn to act shamefully, and not like those that must give account of themselves to God. It is owing to these sins that we have so many wicked boys and girls around us, and that many of the people die in such a miserable way. You know these things are true ; and you must die in the same hopeless manner, except you repent and turn to God. You have had many calls, many seasons of sickness and want ; your sufferings have been great, but they are nothing to the pains of hell. Shall these warnings be lost upon you? Do you wish to die in sin, to be shut out of heaven, and shut up in the bottomless pit for ever ? You say, "I hope not ;" but your hope will be vain, if you do not turn to God. Many go on till death, without repenting of their sins. Do not let Satan deceive you in this way to your eternal ruin. We want to do you good ; we cannot bear to see you so wretched. God does not desire the death of sinners ; Christ died for them ; the Holy Spirit strives with them ; they may be happy in this world and in the world to come. Seek the mercy of the Lord now while it is called to-day. Lead a new life ; and may the Lord give you his blessing and life for evermore.

A PASTOR'S INQUIRIES

ADDRESSED TO THE

COMMUNICANTS OF HIS CHARGE.

PHILADELPHIA:
PRESBYTERIAN BOARD OF PUBLICATION.

A PASTOR'S INQUIRIES

ADDRESSED TO THE

COMMUNICANTS OF HIS CHARGE.

You have, my dear friend, made a solemn profession of religion; and I trust you are indeed what that profession implies, a true Christian. Still, as your spiritual adviser, it is desirable to have some particular knowledge of your views and feelings, aims and hopes in a religious life. The reality, increase, and proper manifestation of your piety, are things in which your pastor feels a deep and fond interest. They are things, also, of infinite importance to you. If I can add to the comfort of your experience, the usefulness of your life, and the preparation of your soul for heaven, it will be an unspeakable blessing to you, and afford the highest gratification to my own feelings. Will you, then, sit down with me to a free and confidential interview on these moment-ous topics; and will you answer each of the following questions according to your best convictions of the truth?

1. Your hope in Christ is a point of chief importance, since on that every thing, in a religious experience, depends. Are your impressions respecting that hope comfortable and encouraging? or do they partake more of uneasiness and distrust? 1 Pet. iii. 15.

2. Do you believe that you have truly repented of sin, and embraced the Lord Jesus by faith, as your Saviour?

3. Do you believe that God, for Christ's sake, has pardoned your sins?

4. After careful examination of your heart by the word of God, do you think it has been renewed by grace? 1 John iii. 21, 14, 24.

5. What are your views of Christ? Does he appear to you a fit and sufficient Saviour?

6. Do you commit your soul with freedom into his hands, and feel a sweet and simple trust in his cross? 2 Tim. i. 12.

7. Do you enjoy communion with him; and does he appear precious to your heart? 1 Pet. ii. 7.

8. Is he the object of tender and lively affections?

9. Do you delight to think of God, as your Father? Rom. viii. 15.

10. Have you the spirit of adoption? are your feelings filial? have you a child-like

dependence on him, love to him, and obedience to his will?

11. When is your hope most comfortable? when you have the most solemn impressions of religion, or when your mind is less occupied with the subject?

12. Do you feel more assurance of your interest in Christ, and more settled peace than you once did? and is it the result of more earnest inquiry, clearer views, and searching application of God's word?

13. Do you seek and cherish the influences of the Holy Spirit, as the means of your sanctification?

14. How long since you professed Christ?

15. Have you realized the hopes and purposes with which you set out in religion? are you as happy as you then expected, and as devoted as you purposed to be?

16. Have you made any sensible progress in religion?

17. Would you now feel satisfied to go on to the end just as you have been thus far; to have your present attainments and comforts, and no more?

18. Is it your desire to grow in grace?

19. Have you a settled aim to become, through Divine grace, all that the gospel is adapted to make you?

20. Are you striving to advance in piety?

21. What means do you employ? 2 Pet. i. 5—8.

22. Have you sought for the causes that

have hindered your progress in holiness? Heb. xii. 1.

23. Do you read the Bible daily with serious attention?

24. Within what period have you read the whole?

25. Have you a relish for the word of God? and do you find its truths and promises adapted to your own experience and your personal necessities?

26. Do you think your knowledge of the scriptures has increased? that you are not only more familiar with its language, but better understand its truths?

27. Do you faithfully attend the sanctuary—not only the Sabbath services, but also as far as possible those of the week?

28. Do you love the worship and ordinances of God? and do you find comfort and benefit in them?

29. Do you daily pray in secret?

30. Have you a time, place, and method of secret devotion? Matt. vi. 6.

31. Do you enjoy this exercise? or do you feel a backwardness to the duty?

32. Do you feel nearness to God, and freedom of utterance in prayer? or does a sense of distance obstruct you in your approach to the mercy seat?

33. Do you feel the importance of a consistent, exemplary Christian deportment before all men? 1 John ii. 6.

34. Do you suppose the secret conviction

of those that know you is, that you are really a Christian ?

35. Would familiar intercourse with you lead an irreligious person to think better or worse of religion ?

36. Do you cultivate a Christian temper ? Phil. ii. 5 ; Col. iii. 12.

37. Do you find it easier to bear and to forgive injuries than you once did ?

38. Are you afraid of backsliding ? and does declension appear dreadful to you ?

39. Do you neglect any known duty ?

40. Are you willing to do whatever God would have you to do ?

41. What are your trials? and how have you borne them ?

42. Do you bring them to God, and plead his promises to the afflicted? and do you feel supported by religion ?

43. What has been the effect of your sorrows ? Have they chastened your heart, and weaned it from earth ? or have they made it more insensible ?

44. When you gave yourself to Christ, was it to be his only, his wholly, and his for ever ?

45. Are you endeavouring to live in the spirit of that covenant ? 1 Cor. vi. 19, 20.

46. Is the cause of Christ dear to you ?

47. Are you doing all you can to promote it by your liberality and your efforts ?

48. Do you give your means systematically, and in strict proportion to your ability ?

49. Do you love the church tc which you

belong, and feel a tender interest in all that affects its welfare?

50. Are you at peace with your brethren?

51. Do you cherish love and fellowship to them as Christ's people? 1 Pet. iii. 8.

52. Do you feel a tender interest in their welfare—long for their holiness—and pray for them? James v. 16.

53. Are you tender of their imperfections and frailties?

54. Do you follow the rule in Matt. xviii. 15, 16?

55. Do you love the souls of men; and feel a great desire that they may be saved?

56. Do you pray fervently for your minister, that his labours may prove a blessing to you and others? 1 Thess. iii. 1.

57. Do you do all you can to bring the unconverted under the means of grace?

58. Are you doing all you can in the Sunday school and otherwise, for the conversion of the young?

59. If all the members of the church were in precisely the same spiritual frame that you are, what would be the state of religion in the church?

60. If they all felt just as you do in reference to the revival of God's work, would you expect a blessing to come?

61. Are your children dedicated to God in baptism?

62. Do you reflect upon the import and solemnity of that transaction—cleave tenderly to the promises of the baptismal cove-

nant, and expect their fulfilment to you and yours?

63. Have you ever explained the meaning of that ordinance to your children, and impressed upon their minds the privileges it confers, and the responsibility it lays upon them?

64. Do you strive faithfully to perform your own engagements in that covenant?

65. Do you carefully instruct your children in the way of salvation—speaking to them solemnly of their sinfulness and their need of salvation, and earnestly persuading them to seek the Saviour?

66. Do you pray for their conversion? in what manner? Do you expect it? when?

67. Is your example adapted to promote their conversion?

68. Do you make it a matter of conscience that they shall keep no company, and engage in no amusements unfriendly to their spiritual good?

69. If they were now to be taken away from you by death, and you could have foreseen that, have you done all that you would have been urged by that foresight to do?

70. If they should never be converted, are you perfectly sure that the loss of their souls would not be owing in any degree to your unfaithfulness?

71. The word of God assigns a prominent place to the departure and final rest of believers. What is the state of your mind on this solemn and interesting subject?

72. Do you live habitually in a state of preparation for a dying hour? Luke xii. 35, 36.

73. Do you ever make the subject of your departure a subject of deliberate meditation?

74. Do you pray for dying grace, a peaceful end, and the Saviour's presence in that fearful hour when flesh and heart shall fail?

75. Are you in bondage to the fear of death? or can you anticipate its approach with a sweet composure?

76. If your last hour were now come, would it find your earthly work done, and your soul meet for heaven?

MARKS OF TRUE SAINTS,

BY

THE REV. J. A. JAMES.

1. When the mind retains its deep solicitude about salvation, and has it increased by the idea, that a lost professor is the most awful of all characters:

2. When there is a continued and increasing dread of sins renounced during concern; and sanctification in these very particulars is carried on with vigour:

3. When besetting sins are, if not totally eradicated, yet repressed and kept under, by watchfulness and prayer:

4. When the idea of being a professor, makes the thought of sin committed more bitter, and renders us restless and uneasy, till we have obtained forgiveness, by renewed faith and repentance:

5. When the sins of others, and especially of professors, and their low state of piety, cause deep grief, and make us additionally anxious to attain to higher degrees of personal godliness, in order that we may preserve the credit of religion, and prevent dishonour from being cast on the name of Christ:

6. When we so love God as to feel that our great business and delight is to obey, serve, and please him; and to find that no measure of service will satisfy us, short of absolute perfection:

7. When the motive to obedience, and to all we do in religion is, so far as we can ascertain it, a prevailing desire and aim to glorify God:

8. When the sins of other professors are matter of grief, humiliation, and distress, and the failings of scripture saints are read with awe, and regarded as beacons to warn us from the rocks on which they split:

9. When we are pleased, not only with comforting preaching, and such as dwells on the doctrines of grace, and privileges of believers, but also with close, pungent appeals to the conscience, and discourses that search the heart and lay open its corruptions, and are ever ready to co-operate with our pastors in promoting revivals of the church:

10. When we retire from earthly minded, fashionable, and lukewarm professors, to associate with those who are eminently holy, consistent and heavenly:

11. When no prospect of gain can induce us to engage in an unlawful occupation; or to carry on a lawful one by forbidden means; and rather than violate truth, honesty, justice and generosity, we would be content with poverty and a quiet conscience.

12. When we carry religion with us into the shop, to regulate all our business, and consider ourselves under solemn obligation to let our light shine forth before worldly men in all our transactions; to make the six days of labour, as well as the one day of rest, a time for glorifying God; and to consider ourselves his servants at all times and in all places:

13. When we feel not only an obligation, but a pleasure, in practising self-denial, and a willingness to give

up the gratifications of appetite and feeling, for the sake of Christ

14. When, though diligent in business, and not careless about property, our chief pleasure in accumulation, is that we have more to do good with: and we avoid luxuries and splendour, that we may have more to spend for God; and while not unmindful of our families, consider that God has claims upon us, as well as they:

15. When we have a tender conscience easily roused, which will not allow us to engage in doubtful actions:

16. When we are as careful to abstain from all angry, resentful and malicious feelings, as we are from licentious and dishonest ones:

17. When our religion is not the spirit of fear, and slavish dread; the service rendered by a slave to a tyrant; but of power, and love, and of a sound mind; the service of a child to a father, in whom he confides, and for whom he has the strongest affection:

18. When there is a strong, steady and laborious desire to do good, especially in the way of converting sinners, by personal exertion, by property, by prayer, so that we feel it to be a part of our calling, and one great end of it to aid in saving souls from death; when we are distressed that little is doing in this way; are willing to make sacrifices to do good; are continually devising means for this purpose; and rejoice in what others are doing, even if they belong not to our party or denomination:

19. When the mind, though not slavishly, or ignorantly anxious about its state, or safety, keeps up a jealous watchfulness over itself, and frequently examines itself before God:

20. When there is in affliction more anxiety to have it sanctified than removed, and a prevailing acquiescence in the will of God in painful circumstances:

21. When the soul feels an habitual drawing to heaven, as to its native country and home:

Then may the professor who has such evidences conclude, that he is indeed a true follower of the Lamb, and not self-deceived.

www.ingramcontent.com/pod-product-compliance
Lightning Source LLC
LaVergne TN
LVHW011218110826
845150LV00006B/1462
* 9 7 8 1 4 2 5 5 1 6 8 5 7 *